Raising Curious Kids

Also by Nancy Sokol Green

Curious and Creative

Raising Curious Kids

Over 100

Simple Activities

to Develop Your Child's

Imagination

Nancy Sokol Green

Crown Trade Paperbacks

New York

For Callan and Kiley, my favorite curious kids

◆

Copyright © 1995 by Nancy Sokol Green

Illustrations copyright © 1995 by Merle Nacht

Published by Crown Trade Paperbacks, 201 East 50th Street,
New York, New York 10022. Member of the Crown Publishing Group.

Random House, Inc., New York, Toronto, London, Sydney, Auckland

CROWN TRADE PAPERBACKS and colophon are trademarks of
Crown Publishers, Inc.

Manufactured in the United States of America

Design by Linda Kocur

Library of Congress Cataloging-in-Publication Data
Green, Nancy Sokol.
Raising curious kids : over 100 simple activities to develop your child's
imagination / Nancy Sokol Green.— 1st ed.
Includes index.
1. Science—Study and teaching. 2. Science—Experiments—Juvenile lit-
erature. 3. Science—Miscellanea—Juvenile literature.
Parent participation. I. Title.
Q181.G765 1994
649'.51—dc20   94-1195
                                                                    CIP

ISBN 0-517-88219-1

10 9 8 7 6 5 4 3 2 1

First Edition

Acknowledgments

Many thanks to my parents, Marvin and Arline Sokol, for inspiring my creativity and challenging me to think; to my husband, Jim, for enthusiastically participating in the activities in this book; and to my editor, Irene C. Prokop, for helping me transform my creative ideas into a simple format for other parents.

Contents

Part II : *Quiet Time*

At Home

Away from Home

On Special Occasions

Author's Note

Simple Activities to Enhance Your
Child's Creativity

When I started observing preschools for my two children, I became concerned that labels such as good, bad, smart, and immature were given to children as young as two years old. Even more disturbing were the criteria from which such labels originated. It appeared that children were only evaluated by their ability to respond to literal learning: in other words, those who could say their ABCs or count to 20 were smart, those who could not perform these tasks were not.

In response to my concerns, I decided to create a weekly class called Curious Kids. I wanted to provide a learning environment where children's creative thoughts, and not their literal thoughts, were emphasized. I didn't think this would be too difficult since I had been presenting countless creative thinking lessons to my students throughout my teaching career. However, I had always taught children who lived in an inner-city environment — children who were not given the opportunity to experience creative outlets such as ballet, music, and art classes. In the past, I had always attributed my students' great enthusiasm for my creative thinking activities to their limited exposure to creative arts experiences, as well as their desire to participate in activities that didn't require grade-level academic skills.

Therefore, I was very surprised to hear equally jubilant responses from the parents and children of Curious Kids. After all, these were not disadvantaged children. In contrast, the children enrolled in Curious Kids came from families who provided numerous opportunities for their children to participate in enrichment classes. Yet these parents often claimed that their children "could hardly sleep the night before Curious Kids." Other parents said their children told everyone that Curious Kids was their "favorite thing in the _whole_ world." By their favorable response, it appeared that these children, too, had discovered something new — something that, despite their academic achievement and numerous extracurricular activities, was missing from their lives.

My experiences have convinced me that all children have incredibly creative minds. Yet if these remarkable minds are not stimulated, we may never discover the wealth of creative thoughts and innovative ideas waiting to surface. Therefore, to help parents unleash, encourage, and enhance their children's creativity, I have written **Raising Curious Kids**.

But chances are your mother or father never encouraged you to season your banana, predict what might happen to a balloon placed in a freezer, decorate your feet, or participate in any of the other bizarre-sounding activities presented in this book. In fact, such activities may seem initially quite strange to you. Yet the out-of-the-ordinary activities in **Raising Curious Kids** have been included for a specific reason. The more bizarre the activity, the less likely it is that a child will search for a preconceived "right" answer. Rather, the child will more likely respond with his or her true creative response. This may be especially important for children who are accustomed to participating in activities that have one correct answer or one way to approach the task.

Also be assured that it is not necessary to have a teaching or educational background in order to implement the activities in this book. This was clearly proven by both the parents of children in the Curious Kids program (who implemented weekly follow-up ideas at home) as well as by my own husband. In fact, my husband will readily tell you that it is not his inherent nature to wear his clothes backwards, whip shampoo in a blender, bathe pennies, or do any of the other activities presented in **Raising Curious Kids**. Yet if you had watched him lead our children in such activities, you would think he had been doing this all his life!

I hope that **Raising Curious Kids** will help parents and their children experience countless hours of fun and creative thinking. I also hope that by participating in a creative thinking environment, both parent and child may discover each other in new and remarkable ways.

After all, when raising curious kids, anything is possible.

How to Use This Book

Getting Started

Raising Curious Kids is divided into two major sections—Part I: Activity Time and Part II: Quiet Time. Part I offers eighty-six hands-on creative thinking activities, while Part II presents over six hundred thought-provoking questions. To begin, you just choose any activity in Part I or ask any question in Part II. It's that simple.

Tips for Creating a
Great Thinking Environment

• Give examples of questions that have no right or wrong answers: What is the best food to eat? What would dog shoes look like? What is your favorite book?

• Emphasize that these kinds of questions do not have just one correct answer. Say how you would like your child to use his or her imagination, ideas, and opinions to answer such questions.

• Avoid praise such as "Great answer!" or "Good idea!" This kind of feedback may encourage children to continue thinking in terms of "I got it right."

• Use praise that focuses on the child's <u>thought process</u>. Examples of such feedback are: "I'm impressed with your thinking." "I'm intrigued by that description." "I liked the way you used your imagination to answer that question."

• Encourage more creative thinking by asking additional thought-provoking questions. Such questions should directly relate to the child's original answer. For example, if a child responds that she would decorate a bike for a princess with jewels, ask more questions about the jewels: "What kind of jewels would you use?" "On what parts of the bike would you put the jewels?" "How will you make sure that the jewels don't become chipped if the princess crashes her bike?"

• If a child does not initially respond to an open-ended question, ask a short series of yes or no questions to help him or her begin the thought process. An example of this kind of questioning is:

> **Parent:** How are salt and sugar alike? How are they different?
>
> **Child:** No answer.
>
> **Parent:** Are they both white?
>
> **Child:** Yes.
>
> **Parent:** Are they both used for food?
>
> **Child:** Yes.
>
> **Parent:** Do they both taste the same?
>
> **Child:** No — sugar tastes sweet.

After asking a few yes or no questions, children will generally then begin to offer some of their own ideas.

• Upon completing creative thinking activities, thank your child for sharing his or her brain with you.

More Creative Thinking

Although the activities and questions in this book ensure many, many hours of creativity, some parents may be interested in creating their own thinking activities as well. To do so, parents can apply the same simple original formulas that were used for the activities and questions in this book. Formula I: Creating Your Own Thinking Activities appears at the end of Part I; Formula II: Creating Your Own Thinking Questions appears at the end of Part II. Formula Practice Exercises, which follow each formula description, help reinforce the major concepts of each formula.

Part I

Activity Time

Activity Time offers forty-three hands-on activities that encourage children to be creative and develop advanced thinking skills. Each of these main activities then leads to another thinking activity, totaling eighty-six activities in all. Activities appear in one of three sections: Let's Experiment, Let's Create, and Let's Decide. Three simple steps — Use the Senses, Do the Activity, and Continue Thinking — are presented under each activity's title.

The materials needed for Steps One and Two (Use the Senses and Do the Activity) are listed at the beginning of the activity. Since your child's ideas are often an integral part of Step Three (Continue Thinking), materials for this step will vary from child to child and, therefore, are not always listed. In most instances, all materials can already be found in the home; a few activities may require that some materials be purchased for minimal cost at local art and teacher-supply stores.

Some parents may wonder why several activities ask children to use and touch food in ways other than what is generally accepted during mealtime. As always, parents should implement only those activities with which they are comfortable. However, parents may want to consider that food has been specifically incorporated into several activities simply because children <u>do</u> have a natural curiosity and interest in exploring what they eat and drink. Moreover, if children are allowed to touch and examine food in creative thinking activities, they may be less likely to play with it during mealtime.

The activities in **Raising Curious Kids** are specifically intended for children aged three to eight. But since creative thinking is not limited to young children, the whole family can be invited to participate. In fact, such participation will greatly enhance the overall thinking environment. For example, family members of different ages will have a different knowledge base, and therefore will respond differently to each open-ended thinking challenge. Such diversity will then stimulate and motivate even more original ideas from all participants. Likewise, young children are more likely to express their own creativity when they observe their parents and older siblings doing the same.

Additionally, since these activities have no set outcome, they can be repeated year after year without children ever becoming bored. How a child might respond to an activity when he or she is five will be very different than at six, seven, or eight. This is because he or she will now have a new set of experiences and knowledge base from which to draw.

Since the activities in the following section can be implemented in any order, just select one — and let the creativity and fun begin!

Let's experiment

◆

Incredible Reactions

Step One
use the senses
◆

Ask your child to compare soda pop with vinegar. Encourage her to use her senses before responding.

example

Which has the strongest smell?
Which is darker in color?
Do the liquids feel different when you touch them?

Step Two
do the activity
◆

Ask your child to predict what will happen if she puts two teaspoons of baking soda into the cup of milk. Allow her to experiment in order to find out. Then ask her what will happen if she

◆

baking soda

5 large glasses, each filled halfway with one of the following: soda pop, vinegar, milk, water, or apple juice

cookie recipe and ingredients

puts two teaspoons of baking soda into the cup of vinegar. Once again, allow her to experiment.

As she watches the vinegar bubble and rise, explain that a chemical reaction between an acid (the vinegar) and a base (the baking soda) is happening. Further explain that all foods are either acids or bases. Ask her to apply this information to explain why the milk did not bubble and rise when mixed with the baking soda.

Next, challenge her to decide which of the remaining liquids are bases and which are acids. Have her predict what will happen to each liquid when baking soda is added. After allowing her to experiment, ask her to compare her predictions with the results.

Step Three
continue thinking
◆

Tell your child that baking soda is used in most cookie recipes. Ask how she thinks cookies would look if baking soda (and baking powder) were omitted from the batter. Make half a cookie batter with baking soda and the other half without it. Ask her to predict what, if any, difference there will be in the cookies after they have been baked. Bake the cookies, and then have her observe the results. Ask her to also evaluate whether or not the cookies from both batters look and taste the same.

Bathing Pennies

You Need

◆

old, dirty pennies

bar of soap

small cloth

¼ cup lemon juice in a small bowl

1 tablespoon salt

one dirty, old nickel

Step One

use the senses

◆

Ask your child to explore the properties of a penny. Encourage her to use her senses before responding.

example

Does a penny roll?

Does a penny bounce?

Does a penny bend?

What else is hard like a penny?

Step Two

do the activity

◆

Ask your child to clean one of the dirty pennies with the bar of soap. Have her scrub it thoroughly, and then tell her to rinse it in the bowl of water. When she has done so, ask her to evaluate the effectiveness of soap and water in cleaning a dirty penny.

Now have her dip the cloth into the bowl of lemon juice, then rub the penny, and observe what happens. Have her compare these results to those she got when she used soap and water.

Continue by adding the salt to the lemon juice. Tell her to drop another old penny into this solution and observe what happens. Ask her to decide which solution is the best for cleaning old, dirty pennies.

Ask if she thinks this solution will work with a dirty, old nickel. Give her one to clean, and have her evaluate this solution's effectiveness for dirty nickels.

Point out that pennies are made of copper. Explain that pennies lose their brightness because copper oxide is formed when the copper combines with the oxygen in the air. Further explain that lemon juice is an acid, and acid — not soap — takes away copper oxide. Using this information, have your child conclude why the solution was not very effective for the dirty nickel.

Step Three
continue thinking

◆

Ask if other acids (such as vinegar or grapefruit juice) would also clean old, dirty pennies. Provide an opportunity for your child to experiment. In conclusion, have her decide which, if any, acid was the most effective.

When Will It Be Juice?

Step One
use the senses
◆

Ask your child to compare frozen grape juice concentrate with grape juice. Encourage him to use his senses before responding.

example

Does the frozen concentrate taste stronger than grape juice?

Does the frozen concentrate smell stronger than grape juice?

How is the frozen concentrate like grape juice? How is it different?

Step Two
do the activity
◆

Help your child put three teaspoons of frozen grape juice concentrate into a large glass. Ask him to predict how many teaspoons of water are necessary

You Need
◆

1 can frozen grape juice concentrate

teaspoon

a large glass

water

1 can frozen orange juice concentrate

to dilute the concentrate before it will taste like the grape juice he usually drinks. After he makes his prediction, tell him to add five teaspoons of water to the concentrate. Then have him smell and taste it. Tell him to continue adding teaspoons of water, then smelling and tasting the juice, until he thinks it tastes like the grape juice he is accustomed to. Keep track of the total number of teaspoons used. When he declares the concentrate has been diluted to taste like juice, compare the actual number used with his prediction.

Now have your child predict how many more teaspoons of water are needed to dilute the juice until it loses its flavor. To find out, have him continue adding teaspoons of water, and smelling and tasting the juice. Keep track of the total number of teaspoons of water used. When your child declares the juice has finally lost its flavor, have him compare the total number of teaspoons of water used with his prediction.

Step Three
continue thinking

◆

Ask whether the same number of teaspoons of water will dilute frozen orange juice concentrate into orange juice. Repeat the experiment with orange juice concentrate. In conclusion, have your child compare the number of teaspoons needed to dilute both concentrates into juice.

Disappearing Ice

Step One

use the senses

◆

Ask your child to explore the properties of ice and to compare it to other things. Encourage her to use her senses before responding.

example

Does an ice cube roll?

Does an ice cube bounce?

What else is as slippery as an ice cube?

What else melts like an ice cube?

Step Two

do the activity

◆

Ask whether it is possible to slow down the melting of an ice cube when it is out of the freezer. Take one cube from the tray and help your child wrap a washcloth around it. Secure it with a

You Need

◆

tray of ice cubes

washcloth

rubber band

aluminum foil

glass of warm water

plate

paper cup

lid of a jar

rubber band. Take another ice cube and help your child wrap it in aluminum foil. Place a third ice cube on a plate, and put the last ice cube in a glass of warm water.

Have your child decide which of the four ice cubes will melt more slowly than the rest. Encourage her to explain why. Then tell her to put her choice for the slowest-melting cube at the front of a line. Have her continue lining up the rest of the cubes, ranking them from the slowest- to the fastest-melting cube. Ask your child to observe and comment on what happens, and to compare the actual results with her prediction.

Challenge your child to think of other ways to slow down the melting of an ice cube. Have her also think of ways that would make a cube melt very quickly.

Step Three
continue thinking

◆

Ask whether the <u>shape</u> and size of an ice cube would affect how quickly or slowly it melts. Help your child pour the same amount of water into a paper cup, into a thick piece of aluminum foil shaped like a flower, and into a lid of a jar. Place all these inside the freezer. When she returns several hours later to take the frozen shapes out of the freezer, ask her to predict which shape she thinks will melt more slowly than the rest. Encourage her to explain why, and then have her observe what happens. In conclusion, ask her to compare the results with her prediction.

Coloring Water

Ask your child to compare a red crayon with red food coloring. Encourage him to use his senses before responding.

example

Which is heavier?

Which has more of a smell?

Which breaks more easily?

Which is brighter?

Step Two

do the activity

◆

Place the jar of water in front of your child. Holding a container of food coloring approximately one inch above the neck of the jar, place a few drops into the water. Have your child observe the results. Then ask whether the water

You Need

◆

food coloring

large glass jar filled with water

red crayon

will color differently if food coloring is dropped from a greater height. Have your child place a different-colored drop into the water, but this time, tell him to hold the bottle eight inches above the neck of the jar. Ask if the effect was different than when the food coloring was dropped from just one inch.

Continue by having your child drop food coloring into the jar from different heights. Encourage him to compare how the relative height of the drops affects the way the water becomes colored. Ask him to also predict what other colors will be created as different colors combine.

Step Three
continue thinking
◆

Ask whether food coloring will react the same way, in different kinds of water (such as hot water, sugar water, or iced water). Provide an opportunity for your child to experiment.

Shampoo in the Mixer

Step One

use the senses

♦

Without identifying it by name, show your child a bowl of unwhipped whipping cream. Ask questions that will help her figure out what it is. Encourage her to use her senses before responding.

example

How does it smell?

How does it look?

How does it feel?

How does it taste?

You Need

♦

whipping cream (that has not been whipped) in a bowl

shampoo

liquid dishwashing detergent

salad oil

orange juice

electric mixer

Now have your child try to name what is in the bowl. After the whipping cream has been correctly identified, turn on the mixer and begin beating it. Ask your child to compare the cream before and after it has been whipped.

Step Two
do the activity
◆

Clean the beaters, and ask whether all liquids change when beaten with an electric mixer. Show her the shampoo, dishwashing detergent, salad oil, and orange juice. Ask her to guess what will happen when each of these liquids is beaten with the mixer.

After she has made her predictions, have her experiment. When she has tried all of the liquids, ask her to compare how each was affected by the electric mixer.

example

Which liquid changed the most? Why do you think that is?
Which liquid changed the least? Why do you think that is?

Step Three
continue thinking
◆

Ask what would result when other liquids (such as vinegar or tea) are mixed with an electric mixer. Provide an opportunity for your child to experiment with the different liquids she suggests.

Don't Freeze!

Step One

use the senses

◆

Ask your child to compare salt, sugar, and cornstarch. Encourage him to use his senses before responding.

example

Which substance has the strongest smell?

Which substance feels the softest?

Which substance tastes the best?

Which substance is the finest?

Step Two

do the activity

◆

Help your child pour equal amounts of water into the paper cups. Then tell him to mix salt in the first cup, sugar in the second, and cornstarch in the third. Label each cup accordingly. After making sure the water in each cup is

You Need

◆

3 tablespoons salt

3 tablespoons sugar

3 tablespoons cornstarch

3 small paper cups

water

spoon

thoroughly mixed, place them in the freezer. Ask your child to predict which, if any, cups of water will not freeze.

example

Will the salt stop the water from freezing? Why or why not?
Will the sugar stop the water from freezing? Why or why not?
Will the cornstarch stop the water from freezing? Why or why not?

Mark down his answers on a piece of paper, and return eight hours later to observe the results. After you have taken each cup of water from the freezer, ask your child questions about what happened.

example

Did the water freeze in all of the cups?
What stopped the water from freezing?
How do you think it stops water from freezing?

Step Three
continue thinking
◆

Challenge your child to think of other substances (such as pepper or baking soda) that might prevent water from freezing. Repeat the experiment using his suggestions.

Bubbling Chalk

Step One

use the senses

◆

Ask your child to compare vinegar with water. Encourage him to use his senses before responding.

example

Which liquid has a stronger smell?

Which liquid is clearer?

Which liquid tastes better?

How are vinegar and water alike?

How are they different?

Step Two

do the activity

◆

Put the two bowls and identical pieces of chalk in front of your child. Ask him to predict what will happen when chalk is placed in water and in vinegar. Then have him put a piece of chalk into each

You Need

◆

chalk

small bowl filled with vinegar

small bowl filled with water

bowl and observe what happens. Ask him to compare the results with his prediction.

Ask if he thinks leaving the pieces of chalk in the liquids for an entire week will make any difference. Have him explain why or why not. In order to find out, label the bowls accordingly and leave the chalk for one week.

Return a week later and have your child observe what happened. Ask him to compare the results with his prediction.

Explain that a chemical reaction has taken place. Further explain that chalk is made out of limestone and that when acid (the vinegar) is in contact with limestone, it breaks apart the calcium carbonate in chalk. Based on this information and the experiment, have your child decide whether or not water is an acid.

Step Three
continue thinking

◆

Ask what other liquids (such as grapefruit juice or lemon juice) might cause chalk to break down after soaking in it for a week. Provide an opportunity for your child to find out. Do not discourage him from experimenting with liquids that are not acids — allow him the opportunity to discover this for himself.

Strange Whipped Cream

You Need

♦

whipped cream in a bowl

raisins

black pepper

vanilla extract

food coloring

shaving cream

cold cream

Step One

use the senses

♦

Put a little whipped cream into the palm of your child's hand. Ask him about properties of the cream and how it compares with other things. Encourage your child to use his senses before responding.

example

How does the whipped cream feel?

What other things feel like whipped cream?

What other things taste as sweet as whipped cream?

Step Two
do the activity

◆

Display the raisins, black pepper, vanilla extract, and food coloring in front of your child. Ask your child to first predict what will happen when each item is dropped into the whipped cream.

example

> Will the black pepper stay on top of, or sink into, the whipped cream? Why?
>
> Will the raisins stay on top of, or sink into, the whipped cream? Why?
>
> Will the whipped cream turn the color of the food coloring or a different color? Why?

Tell your child to hold each item approximately four inches above the bowl before dropping it into the whipped cream. Have him compare what happens with his predictions.

Now ask your child to predict whether or not the results will be different if each item is dropped from a greater height. Have him experiment to find out.

Step Three
continue thinking

◆

Ask your child to predict and experiment with what will happen when these same items are dropped into other creams (shaving cream, sunscreen creams, cold creams). (Be sure to emphasize that these creams <u>cannot be tasted</u>.)

Spinning, Spinning, Spinning

You Need

◆

1 sandwich-size plastic bag

1 grocery-size plastic bag

water

Step One

use the senses

◆

Ask your child to explore the properties of the plastic bags and then compare them to each other. Encourage her to use her senses before responding.

example

Can you make each bag produce a sound?

What other things feel like plastic bags?

Which bag has the strongest smell?

Which bag is thicker plastic?

Step Two
do the activity
◆

Fill the sandwich-size bag about halfway with water, and then spin the top of the bag six times around. Release your hand and have your child observe the speed at which the bag unwinds.

Now have your child predict whether or not the grocery-size bag will unwind faster or slower than the small bag when filled halfway with water. Spin the top of the grocery bag six times, and have your child observe the speed at which the bag unwinds. Have her compare the speed of the two bags.

Then ask whether she thinks the number of twists might alter the results. Repeat the experiment, but this time twist each bag only three times. Ask whether she notes any difference. Repeat the experiment once more, only this time twist each bag twelve times.

Step Three
continue thinking
◆

Ask your child to consider whether the results of the experiment will be different if more or less water is added to each bag. Repeat the experiment several times, filling the bags with different levels of water each time. Have your child decide which size bag and what level of water is best for making a bag unwind with the fastest speed.

A Balloon in the Freezer

You Need

◆

*4 identical bal-
loons*

grocery sack

Step One

use the senses

◆

Ask your child about the properties of
a deflated balloon. Encourage him to
use his senses before responding.

example

How does the outside of the balloon
feel?

How far can you stretch the balloon?

Can you make a sound with the balloon?

Can you fold the balloon in half?

Step Two
do the activity
◆

Blow up the four balloons so that they are identical in size. Have your child place one in the freezer, one in a grocery sack (fold over the top so the balloon cannot be seen), and one on a shelf in a closet. Ask your child to think of one more place to store the last balloon. Place it there, and then challenge him to predict how each balloon will look one week later. Encourage him to support his answers with reasons.

One week later, remove all the balloons from their storage places. Ask your child to decide if some or all of the balloons now look different. Then have him conclude which storage place was the best for keeping a balloon full of air. Encourage him to explain why that place was better than the rest.

Step Three
continue thinking
◆

Ask what other objects (a piece of bread or a leaf, for example) could be stored in a freezer, a grocery sack, and on a shelf for a week. Repeat the activity with the object(s) your child suggests. Have him compare the results of all experiments.

What's That Smell?

Step One
use the senses
◆

Ask your child to compare yeast with sugar. Encourage her to use her senses before responding.

example

Which has a stronger smell?
Which is a darker color?
Which is a finer substance?

Step Two
do the activity
◆

Fill the glass with one-half cup of warm water. Add one teaspoon of sugar

glass

warm water

teaspoon

sugar

package of yeast

basin or large bowl

and stir until it dissolves. Next, have your child add one package of yeast to the glass and stir until it also dissolves. Then set the glass in a basin or large bowl and ask questions about the mixture.

example

What color is the yeast mixture?

How does the yeast mixture smell?

Why are bubbles forming?

Will the yeast mixture get smaller or larger?

Explain that yeast is a living organism. Further explain that the yeast mixture will get larger because carbon dioxide gas is being produced (point to the bubbles).

Ask your child to predict what will happen if yeast is added to warm water <u>without</u> sugar. Allow her to experiment to find out. Finally, ask her to predict what will happen if yeast is added to cold water. Once again, allow her an opportunity to find out.

Step Three
continue thinking
◆

Ask whether more or less carbon dioxide gas bubbles will appear if four teaspoons of sugar are added to yeast and warm water. Encourage your child to explain her answer. Repeat the experiment, substituting four teaspoons of sugar for one. In conclusion, have her compare the results of both experiments.

Drip Drop

Step One

use the senses

♦

Ask your child to compare wax paper, foil, newspaper, plastic wrap, typing paper, and a paper towel. Encourage her to use her senses before responding.

example

Which paper tears the easiest?

Which paper stretches without ripping?

Which paper can make the loudest noise?

Which paper feels the smoothest?

Step Two

do the activity

♦

Tell your child to put one drop of water on each of the following surfaces: wax paper, foil, newspaper, plastic wrap, typing paper, and a paper towel.

You Need

♦

wax paper

foil

newspaper

plastic wrap

typing paper

paper towel

eyedropper

water

soapy water

cooking oil

flat piece of glass

Have her observe and compare what happens to the drop on each of the surfaces.

Next, ask your child to predict whether drops of soapy water will react differently with each surface. Encourage her to explain why or why not. Repeat the experiment once again, using drops of soapy water. Then ask whether drops of oil will react differently than the drops of water. Allow your child to experiment.

Continue by telling your child to put a drop of water, a drop of soapy water, and a drop of oil on the glass surface. Make sure she puts the drops side by side, in a horizontal line at the top of the glass. Ask her to predict which drop will fall the fastest when you lift the glass and why. After she makes her prediction, lift the glass and have her observe what happens.

Step Three
continue thinking

◆

Ask your child what other liquids (such as orange juice, milk, or vinegar) could be dropped on these same surfaces. Provide an opportunity for her to experiment and compare all the results. In conclusion, have her decide which liquid is most readily absorbed on the most surfaces.

Bread Discoveries

You Need

◆

piece of bread

4 zipper-locking sandwich-size plastic bags

masking tape

pen

eyedropper

water

an orange

Step One

use the senses

◆

Ask your child about the properties of bread. Encourage him to use his senses before responding.

example

Can you fold a piece of bread without tearing it?

Can you stretch a piece of bread without tearing it?

Is the crust thicker or thinner at the top?

Step Two

do the activity

◆

Ask whether anything can grow on bread. Then ask whether water and sunshine can somehow affect bread. Encourage your child to support his answers with reasons.

Next, have your child divide the bread into four equal pieces. Tell him to put one piece inside each zipper-locking bag. On a strip of masking tape, write the word "Light," and have your child stick this on a bag. On another piece of masking tape, write "Dark," and have your child label another bag. Ask him to seal them both. Have him place the bag labeled "Light" where sunshine frequently enters the home, and have him place the bag labeled "Dark" inside a closet.

Now tell your child to use the eyedropper to add eight drops of water to each remaining bag. Ask him to seal both bags shut. On different pieces of masking tape, write "Light/Water" and "Dark/Water." Have your child place one of these labels on each bag. Then tell him to place the "Light/Water" bag in the same spot as the one labeled "Light," and the "Dark/Water" bag in the same closet with the one labeled "Dark."

Ask your child to make several predictions about the four bags of bread.

example

Will all the pieces of bread look the same one week later? If so, why?

If not, which pieces of bread will look different? How will they look?

One week later, gather all the bags and have your child note what has happened. Based on his observations, ask your child to decide which conditions are best for growing mold.

continue thinking

◆

Ask whether the results of this experiment would be the same if orange slices, instead of bread, were placed inside the bags. Encourage your child to explain why or why not. Repeat the experiment with an unpeeled orange cut into fourths. In conclusion, have your child compare the results of both experiments.

Backwards Hour

You Need

◆

storybook

dinner

Step One

use the senses

◆

Have your child take off his clothes and then put them back on again — only backwards. Do the same thing yourself. Ask your child questions about how his clothing feels and looks when it is worn this way.

example

Does your shirt feel different? If so, how?

Do you like the way your shirt looks when it is on backwards? Why or why not?

Do your pants feel different? If so, how?

Do you like the way your pants look when they are on backwards? Why or why not?

Step Two

do the activity

◆

Tell your child that he is going to have the opportunity to experience several things "backwards" in the next hour. Ask your child to join you in a countdown (from ten to one) to officially start the hour.

Next, pronounce each family member's name as it would sound if it were written backwards (e.g., Tom/Mot; Jim/Mij). Tell family members that they will be addressing each other this way during the Backwards Hour. Then serve dinner — but start with the dessert as the first course. Continue serving the meal in a backwards order.

After dinner, have your child guess what song you are singing. Sing the lyrics to the song in a backwards order.

example

Lamb little a had Mary

Lamb little a had Mary

Lamb little a had Mary

Snow as white was fleece her.

With your child's assistance, pick another song and then write the lyrics to it in backwards order. Try singing it aloud. Then have your child try walking, running, skipping, and crawling backwards. After each activity, have your child evaluate whether these tasks are more difficult to do this way. Then read one of your child's favorite stories, starting on the last page. Read both the story sequence and sentences of the text in a backwards order. Ask your child to decide how the story's plot was affected by reading it this way.

Step Three
continue thinking

◆

Ask what would be dangerous to do backwards (such as to cross a street or to drive a car on the freeway). Then have your child think of something else he would like to try doing backwards (that is not dangerous). Provide an opportunity for him to do so.

Let's Create

◆

An Unusual Sandwich

Step One
use the senses
◆

Ask your child to compare and evaluate the foods displayed for the unusual sandwich. Encourage him to use his senses before responding.

example

Which food has the strongest smell?
Which food has the sweetest taste?
Which food has the worst taste?
Which food would be the easiest to cut with a plastic knife?

Step Two
do the activity
◆

You Need

◆

hamburger buns

alfalfa sprouts

peanut butter

chocolate chips

raisins

ice cream

cookies

cucumber slices

tomato slices

almonds

potato chips

mustard

whipped cream

plate

plastic picnic knife

Note: *Other foods can also be selected for this activity.*

Ask your child to name ingredients that are generally <u>not</u> used to make a sandwich (such as ice cream, corn, peas, or cereal). Then challenge him to make an unusual sandwich out of some (or all) of the displayed ingredients. Ask your child questions that will encourage him to think creatively while he makes this new sandwich.

example

In an unusual sandwich, could some of the ingredients go on top of the bun?

In an unusual sandwich, could the ingredients be arranged in a pattern (e.g., all in a line, in a circle)?

When your child is finished, ask him to give his creation a name. Then ask him to decide if other children would want to eat this sandwich. Encourage him to explain why or why not. Continue by challenging your child to convince <u>you</u> to try the sandwich (be brave). Finally, ask him if he would like to try his own creation. If so, have your child evaluate how the sandwich tastes to him.

Step Three
continue thinking

◆

Ask what ingredients (such as grated cheese or potato chips) might be unusual in a cookie recipe. Prepare a basic cookie batter and allow him to add some of these ingredients to the batter. Bake the cookies and then have him evaluate how they look and taste.

Glittery Sand

Step One

use the senses

◆

Ask your child questions about the properties of sand. Encourage her to use her senses before responding.

example

Is it easy to hold one grain of sand?
Does sand make a sound if you rub it
between your hands?
How does sand smell?

Step Two

do the activity

◆

Ask whether it might be possible to make sand look like glitter. Encourage your child to explain why or why not. Next, spread out enough newspaper to cover the working area. Ask your child to predict what will happen when she squeezes some food coloring into each

You Need

◆

5 3-oz. paper cups, filled halfway with dry sand

4 different colors of food coloring

4 wooden Popsicle sticks

newspaper

construction paper

glue

cup of sand. Tell her to select a color and to squeeze approximately four to six drops into one of the cups. Using one of the sticks, have her mix the sand until it is colored throughout. Ask her to compare the colored and uncolored sand.

example

Does the colored sand appear thicker?

Does the colored sand appear shinier?

Does the colored sand appear wetter?

Continue by having your child mix each of the remaining colors into one of the cups of sand. For the last cup, have her select <u>two</u> colors to add to the sand. Ask her to predict what color the sand will turn when these colors are combined.

After all the cups of sand have been colored, place squiggly lines of glue all over the construction paper. Have your child sprinkle the "glitter" onto the lines of glue. Then lift the picture and shake off the "glitter" to view the final results.

Step Three
continue thinking
◆

Ask whether sugar or salt could be substituted for sand to make "glitter." Encourage your child to explain why or why not. Repeat the activity, substituting salt, sugar, or any other substance that your child suggests. In conclusion, have her decide which substance worked the best.

Beautiful Feet

You Need

◆

rings

bracelets

necklaces

ribbons (both for hair and presents)

water colors

paintbrushes

stickers of any kind

Step One

use the senses

◆

Have your child compare rings, bracelets, necklaces, and hair ribbons. Encourage her to use her senses before responding.

example

Which ring is the heaviest?
Which bracelet is the brightest color?
Which necklace is the longest?
Which ribbon feels the smoothest?

Step Two
do the activity
◆

Have your child think of body parts (fingers, necks, ears, or wrists) that people ordinarily highlight with different kinds of jewelry. Then ask why people never seem to highlight their feet. Tell your child that, in response to this oversight, her feet are going to be honored today.

Ask your child what she would like painted on her feet (e.g., a rainbow, a sun). Proceed by painting whatever your child requests. Next, using your child's input as to which one and where, place the ribbons, bracelets, and necklaces around her ankles and on top of her feet. Put the rings on her toes. Tell her to place the stickers anywhere on her feet that she chooses. When her feet are completely decorated, ask her various questions about them.

example

Do you like your feet decorated this way? Why or why not? How might your decorated feet be a problem?

Step Three
continue thinking
◆

Ask whether she can think of anything else (such as the bathtub or a garbage pail) that rarely, if ever, gets decorated. Provide an opportunity for your child to decorate whatever she thinks of, using the same or different materials.

An Amazing Dog

Step One

use the senses

◆

Ask your child questions about the properties of glitter. Encourage him to use his senses before responding.

example

Is it possible to pick up one fleck of glitter?

Can you tear glitter? Why or why not?

What materials might glitter stick to without using any glue?

Step Two

do the activity

◆

Tell your child that today he is going to train a new kind of dog to perform whatever tricks he chooses.

Give your child the tagboard strip, crayons, felt pens, glue, and glitter, and

You Need

◆

2-foot-long, 2-inch-wide strip of tagboard

crayons

felt pens

glue

glitter

2 1-inch Velcro strips

3-foot-long piece of yarn

stapler

encourage him to design a collar that dogs would enjoy wearing. When he has finished, staple a Velcro strip to each end of the collar, allowing it to be easily opened and closed. Then staple a piece of the yarn to the collar to be used as the leash.

Explain to your child that you are now going to put the collar and leash around the dog he is going to train. Secure the collar around your neck, get down on your knees and hands, and bark like a dog. Tell your child that it is his responsibility to teach you — as the dog — to sit, heel, roll over, and whatever other tricks he comes up with. After a period of time, switch roles if your child desires.

When the "dogs" have mastered their tricks, invite other family members and friends to come watch the dog show.

Step Three
continue thinking

◆

Have your child imagine that it is possible to train <u>objects</u> in the home to do tricks. Ask him what he would train (e.g., a bed), what he would train the object to do (e.g., make itself), and why (e.g., so he wouldn't have to make it every day).

Painting With Marbles

Step One

use the senses

◆

Ask your child questions about the properties of a marble. Encourage him to use his senses before responding.

example

Where could you drop a marble that would make a loud sound?

Where could you drop a marble that would make a quiet sound?

Do marbles have a smell?

What other things feel like a marble?

Step Two

do the activity

◆

Show your child the marbles and the tennis-ball can and ask whether it is possible to paint with them. Encourage him to explain why or why not. Then

You Need

◆

4 marbles

empty tennis-ball can with a lid

white construction paper cut to fit securely inside the tennis-ball can

4 plastic spoons

4 shallow containers with tempera paint (red, blue, green, and yellow), slightly thinned with water

tell your child that today he will use the marbles and the can to paint a picture.

Place the white piece of construction paper inside the can so that it fits snugly around the entire interior. Then have your child place a different marble in each of the containers of tempera paint. Tell your child to use the spoons to ensure that the marbles are well-coated with paint.

Next, have your child drop each marble into the tennis-ball can. Secure the lid, and have your child vigorously shake the can in all directions for about thirty seconds. Have your child predict what the paper will look like before taking it out of the can. Then take the paper out and ask your child to imagine what he sees in his design.

Step Three
continue thinking

◆

Challenge your child to think of other objects (such as toothpicks or tiny rocks) that could be coated with paint and placed into a tennis-ball can to create a picture. Provide an opportunity for him to experiment with some of his ideas, and then have him compare these paintings to the one made with the marbles and the tennis-ball can.

A Different Band,
A Different Song

Step One

use the senses

◆

Ask questions that will prompt your child to discover how spoons, pans, and cereal boxes can become musical instruments.

example

How can you make a sound using two spoons?

How can you make a sound using the spoon and pan?

How can you make a sound using the cereal box?

do the activity

◆

Challenge your child to think of other objects in the home that could become instruments in a band. Have your child collect these items and show you how a sound can be made from each of them.

Next, have your child select a homemade instrument for both you and her to play. Pick a familiar song and play the "instruments" as you and your child sing along. After you have played a few songs, tell your child that just as band instruments can be original and different, so can lyrics to a song. Demonstrate this by modeling a familiar song with a few changes.

example

(To the tune of "Ring Around the Rosy")
Ring around the bathtub
Ring around the bathtub
Ashes, ashes
We all get clean!

Challenge your child to replace the lyrics of a familiar song with new words as you both play the tune with your instruments.

example

Row, row, row your _____ .
Gently down the _____ .

Merrily, merrily, merrily, merrily,

Life is but a _____ .

◆

Ask what other ways (same words but different tune, for example) a song can be changed. Create a new song using her ideas for modifications. After the song has been created, play it with your homemade instruments.

A Strange Apple Tree

Step One

use the senses

◆

Ask your child to compare aluminum foil, buttons, and sequins. Encourage him to use his senses before responding.

example

Which of these materials tears the easiest?

Which of these materials feels the smoothest?

Which of these materials makes the loudest sound?

Which of these materials is the shiniest?

You Need

◆

apple shapes cut out of white tagboard

crayons

felt pens

aluminum foil

buttons

sequins

glue

3-foot tree made from brown and green construction paper, taped to a wall

do the activity

◆

Have your child recall the part of **Snow White and the Seven Dwarfs** where the Queen (as the witch) gives Snow White the poisoned apple. Have your child imagine that the seeds from this apple fell into the ground, and that a very strange apple tree has now grown where they fell. Tell your child that he is going to make the apples from this tree.

Give your child one of the apple shapes, and challenge him to think about how apples from this strange tree might look. To encourage creative thinking, ask some questions.

example

What color would the apples on this strange tree be? Why?

Could some of the apples have polka dots or stripes on them? Why or why not?

Can you think of ways to use the buttons to make these strange apples?

Can you think of ways to use the foil to make these strange apples?

Provide your child with as many blank apples as he is interested in creating. After he completes each apple, tape or glue it to the green section of the tree on the wall.

Now tell your child that something very unlikely happens (a person begins to sing, for example, or green polka dots appear on one's forehead, or an animal's fur falls off) if a person or animal takes a bite from one of the strange apples. Ask your child to imagine what happens after family members or pets eat one of the strange apples.

Step Three
continue thinking

◆

Ask your child to imagine how this strange apple tree plays a very important part in a sequel to **Snow White and the Seven Dwarfs**. Help him create this sequel and then have him tell it to other family members and friends.

Marshmallow Sculptures

Step One

use the senses

◆

Ask your child questions about the properties of a marshmallow. Encourage him to use all his senses before responding.

example

How does the marshmallow feel?

How does the marshmallow smell?

How far can you stretch the marshmallow?

Can you make a sound with the marshmallow?

Step Two

do the activity

◆

Show your child pictures of sculptures, and ask what materials are usually used to make one. Then tell your child that today he is going to make a sculpture out of marshmallows and toothpicks.

Model how to make such a sculpture by taking one large marshmallow and sticking several toothpicks on different sides. Then place a different-colored marshmallow on the end of each toothpick. Continue adding toothpicks and marshmallows to extend the sculpture both in height and length.

As soon as your child has the idea, give him the marshmallows and toothpicks. After he has finished his creation, ask questions about his sculpture.

example

What does your sculpture look like to you?

What do you call your sculpture?

Where would you like to display your sculpture?

Step Three
continue thinking
◆

Ask your child what other foods (raisins, banana slices, or apple slices) could be placed on toothpicks to make a sculpture. Provide an opportunity for him to make a sculpture using the food(s) he suggests.

Planet Peanut

Step One

use the senses

◆

Ask your child to compare peanut butter with honey. Encourage him to use his senses before responding.

example

Which feels the stickiest?

Which smells the strongest?

Which has the lightest color?

Which leaves a taste in your mouth for the longest period of time?

Step Two

do the activity

◆

Have your child identify what planet he lives on. Then ask whether he has ever heard of Planet Peanut. Tell him that today he will create a creature from this planet.

You Need

◆

1 cup peanut butter

1 cup honey

1 cup dry nonfat milk

raisins

mixing bowl

mixing spoon

Help your child mix together all the ingredients to form a clay and then shape it into a ball. As you explain that the creatures from Peanut Planet are (of course) made from peanut butter, hand your child the ball of clay. Tell your child to use the peanut butter clay and raisins to create a creature from this planet. Remind him that this creature does not have to resemble anything on earth since it comes from a completely different planet.

After your child has created his creature, tell him to name it. Then ask various questions that will prompt your child to infer specific details about his peanut creature.

example

What does it like to eat?

Is it a gentle or wild creature?

Can it communicate any sounds?

Step Three
continue thinking
◆

Ask your child to imagine the kind of home his creature would live in. Gather materials (shoe box, twigs, leaves, building blocks, paper cups, etc.) and help him make a shelter for his peanut creature.

The Grand Tie Exhibit

Step One
use the senses
◆

Ask your child questions about the properties of a tie. Encourage him to use his senses before responding.

example

Does a tie have a smell?
Can you make a sound with a tie?
What else feels like a tie?

Step Two
do the activity
◆

Ask when and where people first had the idea for males to wear ties.

You Need
◆

1 necktie

7 necktie shapes cut out of tag-board

crayons

stickers

sequins

buttons

tissue paper

magazines

glue

scissors

hole punch

string

Then tell your child to imagine that he is now a famous tie designer. Show him the ties cut from tagboard as you explain that his special, unique, and different ties have made him very popular. Further explain that he is about to premiere his best ties at a grand exhibit.

Give your child the materials to decorate the ties. Encourage him to make each tie very unusual (one could have pictures cut out from magazines with sequins on top, another could have crayon and felt-pen designs surrounded by stickers and buttons, etc.).

After the ties have been made, punch a small hole near the top of each tie and thread the string through it. Tie the ends of the string together so that the tie can now be slipped over the head. Put a tie on your child and yourself. Make an exhibit area and display the rest of the ties. Invite other family members or friends to come view the exhibit. Encourage your child to explain why each tie is so special.

Step Three
continue thinking
◆

Ask what things your child owns (e.g., baseball cards, stuffed animals) or has made (e.g., model airplanes, artwork) that could be exhibited. Help him set up a Home Museum to display these objects. Suggest that your child name and label each exhibit (e.g., The Cuddly Collection). Then invite other family members and friends to visit the Home Museum.

A Foot Flower

Step One

use the senses

◆

Ask your child to compare the two flowers. Encourage her to use her senses before responding.

example

Which flower smells the prettiest?
Which flower has the longest stem?
Which flower has the softest petals?

Step Two

do the activity

◆

Show your child the activity materials as you explain that she is going to make a very different kind of flower today. Tell her that this flower will have petals made from shapes of feet.

Begin by having your child take off her shoes. Tell her to place her right foot on the tagboard; trace around her

You Need

◆

2 different kinds of flowers

white tagboard

scissors

crayons

marking pens

pieces of felt

sequins

glue

entire foot. Then have her place her right foot on another part of the tagboard and trace it once more. Repeat the same process for the left foot.

Next, take off your shoes and have your child trace each of your feet two times. Then help your child cut out each traced foot. Have her decorate the foot petals with crayons, marking pens, pieces of felt, and sequins. With your child's assistance, arrange the foot petals to form a flower by glueing each of the petals together. Finish creating the flower by cutting out a stem and leaves, coloring them, and then glueing them to the petals.

Step Three
continue thinking

◆

Ask what other body parts (such as an entire hand, a thumb) could be traced to create petals for an original flower. Repeat the activity with the body part she suggests.

A Mess in a Bag

Step One

use the senses

◆

Ask your child to compare sugar with cornstarch. Encourage him to use his senses before responding.

example

Which has the strongest smell?
Which feels the finest?
Which tastes the best?

Step Two

do the activity

◆

Have your child help you prepare the "mess" mixture. Mix the sugar with the cornstarch in a saucepan. Then add the cold water and heat, stirring constantly until the mixture begins to thicken. Allow the mixture to cool until it is just slightly warm.

You Need

◆

⅓ cup sugar

1 cup cornstarch

saucepan

4 cups cold water

4 bowls

food coloring

8 zipper-locking sandwich-size plastic bags

mixing spoon

Note: *This recipe fills 3–4 sandwich-size bags*

Equally divide the cooled mixture into the four bowls, and add one color of food coloring into each. For darker-colored mixtures, use more food coloring. Mix well. Put each colored mixture into a plastic bag; seal and tape closed. Fill a total of four bags. For extra protection, put each sealed bag inside one more plastic bag and seal shut.

Allow your child time to experiment with the "mess" in the bags by encouraging him to knead, squeeze, and pound it within its plastic casing. Ask questions that will prompt him to observe what happens.

example

What happens to the colors when you knead it?

What happens to the colors when you pound it?

What happens to the colors when you squeeze it?

Does this mixture flatten easily? Why or why not?

Step Three
continue thinking

◆

Ask how the mixture might change if it were heated or frozen. Place one sealed bag into boiling water and another in the freezer. Have your child observe whether any changes occur.

Designs From the Air

You Need

◆

black construction paper

salt

magnifying glass

2 equal pieces of string about 5 inches long

paper cup

Step One

use the senses

◆

Put two grains of salt on top of the black paper and ask your child to analyze them. Encourage her to use the magnifying glass, when needed, as well as her senses before responding.

example

Do both grains of salt look exactly the same?

What other things feel like a grain of salt?

What other things look like a grain of salt?

Step Two
do the activity
◆

Ask how a design could be created on the black paper without ever touching it. Then show your child the black paper, cup, string, and salt. Explain that she is going to use them to make a pendulum that will create such a design.

Make one small hole in the bottom of the cup and two holes opposite each other, about halfway down the side of the cup. Then thread a piece of string through each of the holes in the sides of the cup. Knot one end of each string and tie the two pieces together so that the cup hangs (right side up) from the strings, creating a pendulum.

Put the black paper in front of your child. As your child holds the cup by the string over the paper, pour the salt into the cup. Have your child make different patterns on the paper by slowly swinging the cup back and forth in a pendulum motion. Encourage her to also experiment by swinging the cup in different directions. Ask your child whether she thinks the patterns will change if she raises or lowers the cup as she swings it.

example

Will the pattern change if you swing the cup from a higher height? Why or why not?

Will the pattern change if you swing the cup from a lower height? Why or why not?

Challenge your child to experiment with different heights, and ask her to note how the patterns are affected by raising and lowering the cup.

Step Three
continue thinking

◆

Ask what other things (such as sand or sugar) could be poured inside the cup to make patterns on the black paper. Provide an opportunity for your child to experiment with her ideas.

A New Fish

Step One

use the senses

◆

Have your child compare the brown paper sack, newspaper, and tissue paper. Encourage him to use his senses before responding.

example

Which paper makes the loudest noise?

Which paper has more of a smell?

Which paper feels smoother?

Which paper tears more easily than the others?

Step Two

do the activity

◆

Show your child the picture book of fish, identifying each by name. Ask your child to decide how each fish probably received its name. Then tell your

You Need

◆

picture book of fish

scissors

glue

colored tissue paper

2 identical shapes of a fish cut from a brown grocery sack

sequins, buttons

crayons

felt pens

newspaper

child that a new kind of fish has been discovered in the ocean. As you show him the materials, explain that he is going to create this new and unusual fish. Ask questions that will prompt him to think about how this different fish is going to look.

example

Will your fish have a pattern on it?

Will your fish have bright or dull colors?

Will your fish sparkle?

Place the fish cutouts in front of your child as you encourage him to use some or all of the materials to decorate them. When he is finished, staple the two cutouts together, leaving an opening large enough to stuff the fish with newspaper. Have your child help you stuff the fish until it is full, and then staple the remaining area shut.

Ask your child questions about his new fish.

example

What is your fish's name?

What does your fish like to eat?

What sea creatures like to eat your fish?

Step Three
continue thinking
◆

Ask what besides newspaper (tissue paper or rags, for example) could be used to stuff the fish. Provide an opportunity for your child to experiment with his ideas. Once again, cut two identical fish shapes and staple them together, leaving a small opening. Then have your child try to stuff this fish with whatever material he suggests. When he has done so, ask him to evaluate whether this stuffing was more effective than newspaper. Encourage him to explain why or why not.

Let's Decide

◆

Mom's Shoes

You Need

◆

shoes from
Mother's closet

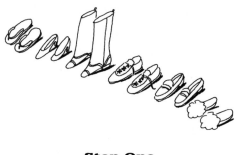

Step One
use the senses
◆

Ask your child to compare two shoes, each from a different pair. Encourage her to use her senses before responding.

example

Which shoe is made from the softest material?

Which shoe can make the loudest noise?

Which shoe weighs the most?

Which shoe has the biggest heel?

do the activity

◆

Ask your child to predict how many pairs of shoes her mother owns. Then ask her to help you take all her mother's shoes out of her closet. Count the number of pairs and put them in the middle of the floor.

As you point to all the different shoes in the middle of the room, ask your child to decide when her mother wears each pair.

example

> When does your mom usually wear her tennis shoes?
>
> When does your mom usually wear her high heels?
>
> When does your mom usually wear her sandals?

Challenge your daughter to decide which pair of shoes is the most comfortable for her mother. Have her put this shoe in the front of a line, and then ask her to continue ranking the shoes from most to least comfortable.

Step Three

continue thinking

◆

Ask what other ways (smallest to largest heel, for example, or oldest to newest) the shoes can be ranked. Have your child rank the shoes again, using her suggested criteria.

Bright Light Hunt

◆

Turn on a lamp and have your child sit or stand near it. Ask questions about the lamp and light coming from it. Encourage him to use his senses before responding.

example

Can you feel the heat coming from the lamp?

Does the shade of the lamp feel softer or harder than the base?

Is the lightbulb hidden or in sight?

Step Two

do the activity

◆

Have your child imagine a home with no lights. To help him do so, turn off all the lights and sit with him in the dark for a few minutes. Ask your child how

You Need

◆

2-×-2-inch squares of blue, red, and yellow paper

tape

his life might be affected if he truly lived in a home without lights.

Then ask your child which lamp or fixture in the home gives off the most light. Show him the colored squares and tell him that he is going to use them to evaluate the brightness of the lights in the house. Explain that he will turn on each light for a few seconds. If the light seems very bright, he will tape a yellow square to the lamp; if it seems somewhat bright, a red square; and if the light is dim, a blue square. For light fixtures that cannot be reached, have him tape the square to the switch that turns the light on.

After all the lamps and fixtures have been tagged, have your child return only to those with a yellow square. Once again, have him momentarily turn on each of these lights in order to determine which gives off the brightest light. Then have him finally decide which light is truly the brightest.

Step Three
continue thinking
◆

Ask what objects in the house are made out of wood. Then challenge your child to decide which of these objects is the largest. Using the same colored squares and coding, have him tag each wooden object. After he has returned once more to the largest objects (tagged yellow), have him decide which is truly the largest wooden object in the home.

Teddy Bear's Birthday

Step One

use the senses

♦

Ask your child questions about the properties of crepe paper. Encourage her to use her senses before responding.

example

Does crepe paper tear easily?

Can crepe paper be stretched without tearing?

What does crepe paper smell like?

Step Two

do the activity

♦

Ask your child how long she has owned her favorite teddy bear. Then ask whether her bear has ever had a birthday party. Tell her that today she is going to plan a party for her favorite bear.

Ask your child to think of birthday

You Need

♦

crepe paper in different colors

construction paper

glue

wrapping paper

scissors

crayons

stuffed animals

decorations that a <u>bear</u> might like. Help your child make and put up these decorations. Then ask your child what should be served at a bear's party. Once again, encourage your child to think about what a <u>bear</u> would like to eat. Last of all, ask what she owns that might be a good present for her teddy bear. With her consent, help her wrap this object.

Begin the party by placing the birthday bear at the head of the table. Place the other guests (the remaining stuffed animals) in the other chairs. Giving directions only when necessary, allow your child to be in charge of the party. Have her lead the games and the birthday song, bring out the party treats, and present her gift.

Step Three
continue thinking

◆

Ask your child whether her teddy bear and other stuffed animals would now like to attend a grand ball (like Cinderella). If so, have your child decide how each animal should be dressed for this special occasion. Then help your child create elegant ballroom attire (such as ties made from shiny paper, capes made from aluminum foil) for each animal that will attend the ball. After all the animals have been dressed, begin the ball. As each animal enters the ballroom, announce its arrival ("Announcing Bunky Bear and his date, Katrina Bear"). Put on some music, and have your child (as well as yourself) dance with the guests.

Food in the Future

Step One

use the senses

◆

Ask your child to compare the different vegetables on the table. Encourage him to use his senses before responding.

example

Which vegetable has the strongest smell?

Which vegetable feels the smoothest?

Which vegetable is the heaviest?

Which vegetable is the largest in size?

Step Two

do the activity

◆

Have your child consider that he may someday be a parent who will decide what his child eats. With this in mind, ask him to group the food on the table into three categories: foods he will never have his child eat; foods he might have his child eat; foods he will certainly have his child eat. When he has finished the task, ask questions that will encourage your child to explain his groupings.

example

Why wouldn't you want your child to eat _____ (point to food)?

Why would you want your child to eat _____ (point to food)?

Why aren't you sure whether or not you will have your child eat _____ (point to food)?

Step Three

continue thinking

◆

Have your child group the food on the table once more. This time, however, challenge him to group the foods into these two categories: food that will still be in the grocery store when he is ninety years old, and food that will no longer be available. When he is finished, ask him to explain why he thinks the food in the latter category will no longer be available when he is ninety.

In a Minute

Step One
use the senses
◆

Ask your child to compare the cooking timer with the wristwatch. Encourage him to use his senses before responding.

example

Which timepiece weighs more?
Which timepiece is louder?
Which timepiece is smoother?

Step Two
do the activity
◆

Ask whether a minute is a long time. Tell your child that both of you will sit absolutely still for one minute, without

You Need
◆

portable cooking timer

wristwatch

crackers

pencil

paper

moving or making a single sound. Set the timer and pass the minute in this manner. Ask whether the minute seemed long or short.

Next, time how long it takes your child to eat one cracker. Tell him how many seconds it took, and then ask him to predict how many crackers he can eat in <u>one minute</u>. Set the timer, and have him begin eating the crackers. At one minute, tell him to stop eating. Compare the number of crackers he ate with his prediction.

Now time how long it takes your child to draw one circle. Tell him how many seconds it took, and then ask him to predict how many circles he can draw in one minute. Follow the procedure used with the crackers: Have him draw circles, stop him after a minute, and then compare the actual number of circles with his prediction.

Challenge your child also to predict how many times he can do each of the following in one minute: stand up and sit down, run around the backyard, and open and shut a door. For each task, follow the same steps previously described.

Step Three
continue thinking

♦

Ask your child to suggest other things (such as somersaults or tying his shoes) he could do in one minute. Allow him to try some of his suggestions. Again, follow the procedure described in the main activity.

The Least
Comfortable Pillow

You Need
◆

pillows

Step One
use the senses
◆

Ask your child questions about the properties of a pillow. Encourage her to use her senses before responding.

example

Does a pillow have a smell?

Can you fold a pillow?

Can you stretch a pillow?

Can you make a sound with a pillow?

Step Two
do the activity
◆

Tell your child to put every pillow in

the house into one big pile. When she has done so, ask her to select the pillow she believes to be the least comfortable. Have her explain why.

Now ask her to arrange the pillows in a line, ranking them from least to most comfortable. When she has completed the task, ask her to explain why she thinks the pillow at the end of the line is more comfortable than the pillow at the beginning of the line (the least comfortable).

Next, have her ponder whether a dog would rank the pillows in the same order that she did.

example

Would a large or small pillow appeal to a dog? Why?

Would a soft or hard pillow appeal to a dog? Why?

Once again, challenge your child to rank the pillows from least to most comfortable, only this time from a dog's perspective. When she has completed the task, ask her to explain why she thinks a dog would like the pillow at the end of the line (the most comfortable) and not like the pillow at the beginning of the line (the least comfortable).

Step Three
continue thinking

◆

Challenge your child to think of other ways (such as by size or from most to least colorful) to rank the pillows. Have her rank them according to her suggested criteria.

Raisin Decisions

Step One

use the senses

◆

Ask your child to compare the raisins with other foods and objects. Encourage her to use her senses before responding.

example

What tastes sweeter than a raisin?

What smells sweeter than a raisin?

What is softer than a raisin?

What is stickier than a raisin?

Step Two

do the activity

◆

Have your child name foods that have raisins in them. Ask her to decide whether these foods taste better because of the raisins. Encourage her to explain why or why not.

Now tell your child that she is going to make several predictions about raisins. First, ask her to first decide whether identical boxes of raisins have the exact same number of raisins inside. To find out, help your child count the raisins in both boxes. Have her note whether her prediction was correct. Then ask whether she thinks every raisin looks exactly the same. Challenge her to compare two raisins to see if she can find any differences.

Next ask her to decide whether it is possible to stick two raisins together without using glue or tape. Have her experiment and note the results. Then ask whether it is possible to stick two raisins together after they have been dipped in cooking oil. Once again, have her experiment and note what happened.

Continue by asking whether raisins melt. Drop a few raisins in boiling water and have her observe. Finally, ask whether a boiled raisin will taste different from an uncooked raisin. Encourage her to explain why or why not, and then allow her to taste both kinds of raisins.

Step Three
continue thinking
◆

Ask if the results of the experiments would be different if peanuts were used instead of raisins. Provide an opportunity for her to experiment with two identical bags of peanuts. Follow the same procedures, and ask the same questions, only this time, have your child predict what will happen with peanuts. In conclusion, have her compare these results with those of the raisin experiments.

The Most Fragile Toy

Step One
use the senses
◆

Ask your child to explore and compare the properties of the toys. Encourage him to use his senses before responding.

example

Which toy is the longest in size?

Which toy makes the loudest sound?

(Point to any toy.) What might be a new and different way someone could use this toy?

Step Two
do the activity
◆

Ask your child to decide which of his toys break more easily than others. Then ask him to choose a total of ten toys that together represent those that do and those that do not break easily. Have him put them in the middle of a room.

Now challenge your child to place his toys in a line from most to least fragile. Begin by asking him to select the toy he believes is most fragile. If he needs assistance, ask questions that will prompt him to rate each toy by its probability of breaking or tearing.

example

(Point to a toy) Will this toy break more easily than the others if it is dropped?

(Point to another toy) Will this toy tear more easily than the others if I pull on it?

When your child has completed ranking his toys, encourage him to explain how he decided on his order.

Step Three
continue thinking
◆

Challenge your child to think of other things in the home (such as a vase or a coffee cup) that are fragile. Help him carefully gather these items and tell him to place them on a carpeted area. Challenge him to rank the objects from most to least fragile.

Some Spicy Sauce

Step One

use the senses

◆

Sprinkle a little of each spice on a plate and ask your child to compare them. Encourage her to use her senses before responding.

example

Which spice smells the sweetest?

Which spice smells the strongest?

Which spice tastes the worst?

Which spice tastes the best?

Step Two

do the activity

◆

Challenge your child to name the spices in front of her, then identify those that she does not know. Next, show your child the corresponding container for each spice. Using the contain-

You Need

◆

a variety of spices, including garlic powder, thyme, red pepper, cayenne, dill, salt, and basil

plate

3 small bowls of unseasoned tomato sauce

ers, have her rank the spices from most to least spicy.

Continue by having her taste the unseasoned tomato sauce and comment on its flavor. Then tell her that she is going to use spices to add more flavor to the bowls of sauce. Explain that she will be making three different sauces — a mildly spicy sauce, a sweet-spicy sauce, and a very hot-spicy sauce. Before she begins, ask questions that will prompt her to apply her knowledge of spices to make these different sauces.

example

Which spices will make the sauce taste sweet?

Which spices will make the sauce taste hot?

How much red pepper will make the sauce taste very hot?

Encourage your child to gradually add small amounts of each spice, pointing out that she can always add more but cannot take away whatever she has already added. As she creates the three sauces, have her continually taste each to determine whether it needs more spices. When she is finished, have her decide which is her favorite and why.

Step Three
continue thinking

◆

Have your child think of foods and drinks (milk, cereal, or bananas, for example) that are typically not seasoned with spices. Allow her to taste any of these foods or drinks with various spices added. In conclusion, have her evaluate how each food or drink tastes after it has been seasoned.

House Dress-up

You Need

◆

shirts

pants

socks

shoes

scarves

necklaces

ribbons

hats

mittens

Step One
use the senses

◆

Ask your child to compare different necklaces. Encourage her to use her senses before responding.

example

Which necklace is the longest?

Which necklace is the shiniest?

Which necklace is made of the smoothest material?

Step Two
do the activity

◆

Ask your child to help you select shirts, pants, shoes, scarves, necklaces, hair ribbons, hats, and mittens from your wardrobe and hers. Then tell your child that today she is going to play dress-up somewhat differently — she will be dressing up a room in the house.

Decide which room will be dressed. Now have your child decide which objects in the room will be dressed, as well as which article of clothing each object will wear (e.g., socks on the TV antenna, a scarf around a lamp, shoes on the leg of a chair). Help your child dress these objects as you ask why she has selected certain articles of clothing for specific objects.

example

Why might antennas like to wear socks?

Why did you pick the legs of the chair to wear the shoes?

Keep in mind that nonfurniture items (doorknobs, curtain rods, or telephones) can also be clothed. After everything is dressed, ask whether or not people might ever really dress objects in their home. Encourage your child to explain why or why not.

Step Three
continue thinking
◆

Have your child think of other objects (such as a tree or a bicycle) that are never dressed. Provide an opportunity for her to dress these objects.

Bean Cookies

Step One

use the senses

◆

Ask your child to compare the cookie cutters. Encourage him to use his senses before responding.

example

Are the cookie cutters the same weight?

Which cookie cutter is made of the strongest material?

Which cookie cutter has the most edges?

Step Two

do the activity

◆

Take one of the cookie cutters and demonstrate how to trace its shape on paper. Show your child the beans, and ask him to predict how many beans will fill the area inside the traced

You Need

◆

paper

cookie cutters in different shapes

kidney or lima beans

pencil

cookie-cutter shape. After he has made his prediction, have him fill in the area, counting each bean aloud. When the entire area has been filled, have him compare the actual total number of beans used with his prediction.

Continue by having your child trace the shapes of the remaining cookie cutters. Follow the same procedure for estimating and then determining the number of beans needed to fill in the area of each cookie-cutter shape.

When the areas of the traced cookie cutters all have been filled, ask questions that will prompt your child to reflect upon his estimations.

example

What did you think about before you made each guess?

Was it difficult or easy to guess the number of beans?

Which shape was the most difficult to guess the number of beans? Why?

Step Three
continue thinking
◆

Ask what other objects in the home (such as the bottom of a glass or a shoe) could be traced on paper. Provide an opportunity for your child to trace these objects. Repeat the activity, filling the area(s) of the newly traced object(s) with beans.

Favorites

Step One
use the senses
◆

Place one of the toys in your child's hand. Tell her to close her eyes and imagine that she is blind and has never seen this toy. Challenge her to use only her sense of touch to describe the toy. If necessary, ask questions to help her.

example

Does the toy feel smooth?
Does the toy feel heavy?
What shape does the toy feel like?

Then have your child close her eyes once more. Put another toy in her hand and have her use only her sense of touch to guess its name.

Step Two
do the activity
◆

Have your child select ten of her

You Need
◆
toys

favorite toys and put them in the middle of a room. Ask her which of the ten is her very favorite toy. Have her explain why, and then put that toy at the beginning of a line. Now tell your child that you are going to guess how she would rank the remaining toys in the pile, from most to least favorite. Tell your child not to comment as you place these toys in the order you believe to be correct.

When you are done, ask whether the order represents how she would have ranked the rest of her toys. Have her change the position of any toys that are not in her preferred order.

Step Three
continue thinking
◆

Have your child think of a friend, relative, or famous star. Challenge your child to rank the toys from most to least favorite as she believes the friend, relative, or star would.

Stacked High

You Need

◆

books of different sizes

Step One

use the senses

◆

Ask your child to compare and explore the properties of books. Encourage her to use her senses before responding.

example

Which book is the heaviest?

Which book is the lightest?

Do different books have different smells?

What kinds of sounds can a book make?

Step Two
do the activity
◆

Ask your child to show you her thigh. If she does not know where it is, show her. Now ask her to predict the number of stacked books needed to reach the height of her thigh.

To find out, help her gather a large pile of books in the center of a room. Challenge her to put the books in a line from the largest to the smallest. Starting with the largest, have your child stand still as you begin to stack the books next to her. Encourage your child to count out loud as you stack each book. When the books have finally been stacked to her thigh, have your child note whether she predicted that more or fewer books would be needed.

Now ask her to predict how many books would be necessary to reach <u>your</u> thigh. Once again, line the books up from largest to smallest, but this time, have your child stack the books until they reach your thigh. Have her compare her prediction with the actual number of books needed.

Step Three
continue thinking
◆

Challenge your child to think of other objects (blocks, pillows, or folded towels) that could be stacked to measure the distance from the floor to her thigh. Repeat the activity using your child's suggestions.

Don't Take Away
My Spoon!

Step One
use the senses
◆

Ask your child to compare utensils.
Encourage her to use her senses before
responding.

example
Do all the utensils weigh the same?
Do all the utensils feel the same?
Which utensil is the longest?
Which utensil is the widest?

Step Two
do the activity
◆

Ask your child to imagine that suddenly people are allowed to use only
one kitchen utensil for the rest of their
lives. Have her decide which utensil she
would pick and why. Then ask her to
guess which utensil you would pick and

You Need
◆

fork

spoon

knife

spatula

soup ladle

peeler

why. After she has given her reason, tell her your choice and provide your explanation.

Next, ask her to imagine various alternatives that people could use if specific utensils truly no longer existed.

example

What else could be used to scrape a carrot?
What else could be used to dish out soup?
What else could be used to flip pancakes?

Continue by challenging your child to place the kitchen utensils in order of most to least important. Ask questions that will prompt her to elaborate on her thought process.

example

Why is a scraper less important than a soup ladle?
Why is a fork more important than a spoon?

Step Three
continue thinking
◆

Ask if it would be possible to eat soup or ice cream with a fork, cut an apple or banana with a spoon, dish soup out with a spatula, and so forth. Provide an opportunity for your child to experiment. Have her evaluate the effectiveness of each utensil when used in a nontraditional manner.

Formula I:

Creating Your Own Thinking Activities

By following the same simple formula used in Part I, you can also become empowered to create your own thinking activities. The three basic steps to this formula are:

Step One: use the senses

Step Two: do the activity

Step Three: continue thinking

Various kinds of creative thinking questions are asked for each step of Formula I. They are as follows:

Step One:

Use the Senses

Ask children to respond to three to five questions that prompt them to use their senses (sense of touch, smell, taste, hearing, sight) about some or all of the materials used in the upcoming thinking activity. Children can:

Compare   Describe and/or evaluate how objects are alike or different upon smelling, tasting, hearing, seeing, or touching them.

Example: Which ribbon feels the smoothest?

Reveal   Examine materials more closely.

Example: How does glitter look under a magnifying glass?

Explore   Experiment to discover whether an object can roll, bend, tear, bounce, stretch, or make a sound.
Example: Can you stretch a penny?

Explain   Tell how an object feels, smells, tastes, sounds, or looks.
Example: How does vinegar taste?

Keep going   Ponder what other things feel, smell, taste, look, and sound like the object.
Example: What else feels like a grain of salt?

These five different kinds of questions can be easily remembered by referring to the acronym CREEK (Compare, Reveal, Explore, Explain, Keep Going).

Step Two:
Do the Activity

Present an activity that stimulates original thought and imagination. Activities can include one or more of the following:

Creations   Create something different out of familiar objects.
Example: How could we use marbles to paint a picture?

Opinions   Evaluate something from a personal perspective.
Example: What do you think is the best way to arrange your room?

Experiments Explore what could happen when familiar objects are placed in different situations.
Example: What will happen if we soak an old penny in lemon juice?

Decisions Decide or rank something by a specific criteria.
Example: How would your mother rank her shoes from most to least comfortable?

The four categories for the different kinds of activities can be easily remembered by referring to the acronym COED (Creations, Opinions, Experiments, Decisions).

Step Three:

Continue Thinking

Thinking activities never really end. Instead, each activity is just a springboard for more creativity. Activities can continue if you:

Add Do the same general activity again — but add different ingredients or materials.
Example: What could be added to make the paint sparkle?

Repeat Do the exact same activity again — but from a different person's perspective.
Example: How would a dog rank these pillows from most to least comfortable?

Omit Do the same general activity again — but omit an ingredient or material.

Example: Will the cake still rise if we don't use baking soda?

Substitute Do the same general activity again — but substitute different amounts or kinds of ingredients and materials.

Example: Will the results be the same if we use four tablespoons of sugar instead of two?

Explore Think how other places, approaches, or conditions might affect the activity.

Example: Will the result of this experiment be the same if we do it in the dark?

These variations can be easily remembered by referring to the acronym A ROSE (Add, Repeat, Omit, Substitute, Explore).

Practice

The following exercises will help you become more familiar with Formula I. Although the words in the blank spaces of the exercises will change, these basic questions can be asked over and over again.

Have fun as you try the exercises. And remember — there are no wrong answers!

Exercise I:

use the senses

These kinds of questions (e.g., Can you make a sound with your socks? Can you bend your shoes? What does Play-Doh smell like? Which of your crayons is the shortest? What else feels like your blanket?) can be asked throughout the day.

To think of ways to uses the senses, recall things that your child plays with, enjoys, or is interested in. Write these ideas and more in the blanks below.

Example: Which <u>of your sand toys</u> makes the loudest noise?

Comparing Questions

Which _____ feels the smoothest?

Which _____ has the strongest smell?

Which _____ feels the heaviest?

Which _____ tastes the best?

Revealing Questions

How does _____ look when held up to the light?

How does _____ look when you put it under a magnifying glass?

Exploring Questions

Can you make a noise with a _____?

Can you tear _____?

Can you stretch _____?

Can you bend _____?

Can you bounce _____?

Can you roll _____?

Explaining Questions

What does _____ smell like?

What does _____ feel like?

What does _____ look like?

What does _____ taste like?

What does _____ sound like?

Keep Going Questions

What else feels like _____?

What else looks like _____?

What else tastes like _____?

What else sounds like _____?

What else smells like _____?

Exercise II:

do the activity

These kinds of questions (e.g., How could you make a cape for your teddy bear? How could you decorate your wagon? Could toothpaste work like glue in an art project? How would you group the shoes in your closet? What could you make out of an empty paper towel roll? How would a drawing look if you put a crayon in both hands to color?) are the basis for original creative thinking activities throughout the day. (Remember, questions from the Use the Senses step are also asked prior to beginning any of these activities.)

To think of creative activities, recall things that your child plays with, enjoys, or is interested in. Fill in the blanks below with these ideas and more.

Example: How would you decorate <u>a bike</u> for a witch?

Creating Questions

What could we make out of _____?

What could be added to _____ to make it look pretty?

How could we make a _____ look different?

Opinion Questions

What is the best way to make _____?

What is the easiest way to _____?

What would make _____ more fun?

Experimenting Questions

What will happen if we add _____ to this recipe?

What will happen if we put _____ in the freezer?

What will happen if we _____ the dark?

Deciding Questions

How would you rank _____ from most to least expensive?

How would you rank _____ from softest to smoothest?

How would you make a _____ for a king?

Exercise III:

continue thinking

These kinds of questions (e.g., What could you add to your sandwich to make it tastier? How would your teddy bear sing that song? What other ways can you use this toy? What else could you use a spoon for? Will this game be different if we close our eyes while we play?) can be asked after a routine activity or as an extension of any thinking activity.

Recall things your child plays with, enjoys, or is interested in. Fill in the blanks below with these ideas and more.

Example: How would <u>your father</u> rank these foods from most to least healthy?

Add Questions

What would be strange to add to _____?

What could we add to _____ to make it shinier?

Repeat Questions

How would a _____ decorate this project?

How would _____ rank your toys from most to least fun?

Omit Questions

Will the results be the same if we don't use _____?

Can we still make a _____ if we don't use scissors?

Substitute Questions

Will the results be different if we use double the amount of
_____?

Could we use food color instead of _____ to do this project?

Will the project look the same if we put it in the _____
_____?

Will the results of the experiment be different if we do it in the _____?

Part II

Quiet Time

In Quiet Time, over six hundred creative thinking questions are presented. Unlike literal questions that require one correct answer, these questions challenge children to respond with their own creative thoughts. Therefore, any answer is acceptable.

The questions in this section appear under one of the following four headings:

> Let's Ponder (questions whereupon children wonder about the origins of events, inventions, words, customs, and what changes may take place in the future)
>
> Let's Compare (questions whereupon children recognize similarities and differences between objects and actions)
>
> Let's Decide (questions whereupon children make a decision and support their answer with reasons)
>
> Let's Imagine (questions whereupon children offer their own ideas about unusual and different situations)

These questions have also been divided into three general sections. They are: At Home, Away from Home, and On Special Occasions.

Each of these sections can be utilized in a variety of ways. First, children frequently find themselves waiting for something to happen — a friend to come over, a doctor to enter the examining room, a birthday party to begin. These waiting periods, which often seem endless to children, can be an excellent time to ask creative thinking questions.

Such questions can also help pass the time more quickly during routine activities (taking a bath, shopping at the grocery store) that some children may not enjoy. Creative thinking questions can also be helpful when children are nervous (a baby-sitter is arriving, a visit to the dentist) or upset about doing something (going to bed, picking up a mess).

Additionally, creative questions provide an opportunity for parents and children to have meaningful communication with each other. With such questions, parents do not have to pretend to listen as their children "babble" away on a topic, nor do children have to pretend to listen to their parents while they are really daydreaming. Instead, such questions motivate and interest both parents and children to listen and respond to each other's original thoughts.

Since there are no right or wrong answers to creative questions, children and adults of all ages can respond. However, to do so, a literal knowledge of the question's topic is needed by the person responding. For example, children living in warm climates may not be able to answer questions about snow simply because they have never felt, seen, or played in it. Therefore, each parent will need to decide which questions may or may not be appropriate for their own children.

Please also note that the questions appearing under each topic in the At Home, Away from Home, and Special Occasion sections not have to be presented only during these times.

These questions can also be included in any general thought-provoking conversation you have with your child.

By responding to questions that have no right or wrong answers, children may be better prepared as adults when confronted with the complicated, open-ended questions that life presents, such as: Which is better — a fixed or variable loan rate? What is the best car to buy for this amount of money? Should I buy life insurance? Last of all, after asking creative questions over a period of time, do not be surprised if your child begins asking you to respond to some of his or her own questions. In a true thinking environment, anyone can respond — and anyone can do the asking!

At Home

◆

Getting Dressed
◆

Let's Ponder

What would dog shoes look like?

How do you think socks got their name?

Why don't we say we "got pantsed" instead of "got dressed" when we put on pants?

Why isn't a nightgown called a <u>morninggown</u> when a person awakens?

What else besides clothing has zippers?

What else could you wear to keep dry if you didn't have a raincoat?

Why do some kids argue about getting dressed?

Let's Compare

How are a sweater and a blanket alike? How are they different?

How are shoes and socks alike? How are they different?

How is getting dressed like wrapping a gift? How is it different?

Let's Decide

Would animals like to wear shoes? Why or why not?

Do people all over the world wear pajamas? Why or why not?

Which is easier to do — zip or button a jacket? Why?

Which article of clothing is the most difficult to put on? Why?

Which article of clothing is the most important? Why?

What is your worst outfit to wear? Why?

Who should pick what you wear each day? Why?

Let's Imagine

You own a very strange bathing suit. What happens every time it gets wet?

You have just been introduced to a Thunk-a-munklunk. What is it wearing that humans would never wear?

Design a party outfit for the space creature Shoo-loo-loo. What does it look like? How is it different than party outfits worn on earth?

At Mealtime

◆

Let's Ponder

What would Big Bird like to eat for breakfast?

What would a king like to eat for breakfast?

What else is as cold as ice cream?

What is hotter than soup?

Which foods take a long time to grow? Why?

What would be very strange to put in your cereal?

How would you get your child to like vegetables?

Let's Compare

How are salt and sugar alike? How are they different?

How are breakfast and dinner alike? How are they different?

How are eating and drinking alike? How are they different?

Let's Decide

What is the best food to eat?

What is the worst food to eat?

Do dogs like candy as much as kids? Why or why not?

Would you be willing to try green milk? Why or why not?

Should kids have to eat foods that they do not like? Why or why not?

Will people still be eating the same food one hundred years from now? Why or why not?

Which food do you think is eaten most often by people all over the world?

Let's Imagine

You are at a birthday party on the planet Zigmifflacky. What do they serve at parties on this planet?

You are the owner of the world's most popular restaurant for kids. What makes your place so special?

The world's most famous chef is going to make you dinner. What will you ask him to make?

Cooking in the Kitchen

◆

Let's Ponder

What would Cinderella cook for her stepsisters and stepmother?

How could a person get hurt while cooking?

What else besides cooking can you do in a kitchen?

What will kitchens look like one hundred years from now?

What makes a good cook?

Why do you think humans — but no other animals — cook their food?

Why don't some people like to cook?

Let's Compare

How are cooking on a barbecue and cooking on a stove alike? How are they different?

How are chopping vegetables and chopping wood alike? How are they different?

How are grated cheese and grated carrots alike? How are they different?

Let's Decide

What is the most difficult food to cook? Why?

What is the easiest food to cook? Why?

What would you like to learn how to cook?

Do you like to help with the cooking? Why or why not?

Who should do the cooking in the house? Why?

Do you think famous people ever cook for themselves? Why or why not?

Could a blind person ever be a great cook? Why or
why not?

Let's Imagine

On the planet Zala Mala, they do not use pans for
cooking. What do they use them for?

You have created a new breakfast cereal for karate
champions. What ingredients did you use?

You tried to cook dinner, but everything went wrong.
What happened?

Picking Up a Mess

◆

Let's Ponder

Why don't most kids like to pick up their mess?

How could you make cleaning up fun?

How did people sweep up their mess before brooms
were invented?

What might be good about having a clean room?

How could a messy room be unsafe?

What rules would you make about cleaning up if you
were a parent?

What would you do if your children did not follow
these rules?

Let's Compare

How are cleaning your room and cleaning yourself
alike? How are they different?

How are litter on the beach and a messy room alike?
How are they different?

How are cleaning up your room and cleaning up the planet alike? How are they different?

Let's Decide

Is a clean room important? Why or why not?

Should parents have to clean up a mess made by their kids? Why or why not?

Should kids get into trouble if they do not clean up their mess? Why or why not?

When should a mess be cleaned up?

What was the worst mess you ever had to clean up?

Are most adults neater than most kids? Why or why not?

Are most girls neater than most boys? Why or why not?

Let's Imagine

You own a toy-picker-upper. What does it look like? How does it work?

You have not cleaned your room for one entire year. What does it look like?

You have just seen a bed that makes itself. Convince your parents to buy it for you.

When a Friend Comes Over

◆

Let's Ponder

What famous people would you like to be friends with? Why?

What might you tell a friend that you would not tell a parent?

What might a friend do that would make you sad?

Why do some people seem to have more friends than
others?

Why do friends sometimes fight with each other?

What will your best friend and you do together when
you are old?

How will your best friend look when he or she is
eighty years old?

Let's Compare

How are a best friend and a favorite teddy bear alike?
How are they different?

How are having friends and having pets alike? How
are they different?

How are your friends alike? How are they different?

Let's Decide

Do cats become friends with other cats? Why or why
not?

Could a plant be a friend? Why or why not?

Would Goldilocks have wanted to be friends with
Little Red Riding Hood? Why or why not?

Could the three little pigs and wolf ever have become
friends? Why or why not?

What is the best thing a friend can do for another
friend?

What is the worst thing a friend can do to another
friend?

What makes a good friend?

Let's Imagine

You are the creator of the award-winning Friendship
Soup. What are the ingredients?

Your best friend has just moved away. What do you write him or her in your first letter?

Your friend calls you a "chicken" when you won't do something you think is dangerous. How will you answer your friend?

When a Parent's Friend Comes Over

◆

Let's Ponder

What do parents say that makes you think they have forgotten what it's like to be a kid?

What might frighten a parent?

What would be strange for a parent to wear? Why?

What would surprise you to see a parent doing? Why?

Why do some kids always bother their parents when their parents' friends are over?

What do parents like to do with their friends?

What else are parents responsible for besides their children?

Let's Compare

How are your mom's best friend and your mom alike? How are they different?

How are parents and kids alike? How are they different?

How are animal parents and human parents alike? How are they different?

Let's Decide

How often should parents visit with their friends?

Which parent rules are unfair to kids? Why?

Should parents ever have "time out" for a behavior that kids do not like? Why or why not?

Would your mother want to be friends with Minnie Mouse? Why or why not?

Would your father want to be friends with Superman? Why or why not?

Would you like to be a parent when you get older? Why or why not?

What is the most difficult thing about being a parent? Why?

Let's Imagine

You are in charge of a party for your parents and their friends. What will you plan for them?

You are the parent. How will you get your children to go to bed when your friends are visiting?

You are the parent. How will you get your child to stop whining when your friends are visiting?

Watching Television

◆

Let's Ponder

Where would be a very strange place to find a TV?

What are some other things to do besides watching TV?

What things are heavier than a TV?

What things are lighter than a TV?

What do you think cave dwellers would think a TV is?

What kinds of programs would you allow kids to watch? Why?

What kinds of programs would you not allow kids to watch? Why?

Let's Compare

How are reading a book and watching TV alike? How are they different?

How are watching TV and watching a play alike? How are they different?

How are videos and TV programs alike? How are they different?

Let's Decide

Do animals watch TV? Why or why not?

Is it good for kids to watch TV? Why or why not?

Should parents tell their kids which TV shows they are allowed to watch? Why or why not?

What is your favorite TV show? Why?

Would you like to be on a TV show? Why or why not?

Do you like to watch commercials? Why or why not?

Who watches more TV — parents or kids? Why?

Let's Imagine

You are on a TV commercial. What are you selling? What do you say and do in the commercial?

Number 7 is now a magical channel on your TV.

What happens every time you push this channel?

Now that you are ninety years old, you find that TVs have changed quite a bit over the years. What do they look like? How do they work?

Before the Sitter Arrives

◆

Let's Ponder

Why do some kids like to break the rules when a sitter is in charge?

How do you think the word <u>baby-sitter</u> became part of the language?

What other words could be used to describe people who take care of kids when their parents are not home?

What should parents know about a sitter before allowing him or her to take care of their kids?

Why do some kids become shy when the sitter arrives?

What might make a baby-sitter nervous?

What would your students learn if you were the teacher at a baby-sitting school?

Let's Compare

How are dog-sitting and baby-sitting alike? How are they different?

How are baby-sitters and nurses alike? How are they different?

How are baby-sitters and parents alike? How are they different?

Let's Decide

What makes a good baby-sitter?

At what age should kids begin baby-sitting?

Should kids or parents pick who will baby-sit? Why?

Should baby-sitters have to take a first-aid course? Why or why not?

Should baby-sitters tell the parents if the kids did not cooperate? Why or why not?

What should happen to kids who do not listen to the baby-sitter?

What should happen to baby-sitters who do not listen to the parents' instructions?

Let's Imagine

Your new baby-sitter has arrived wearing something very strange. What is the sitter wearing, and why?

You are the baby-sitter and the child refuses to go to bed. What are you going to do?

You are the baby-sitter and the child has not stopped crying since her parents left. What are you going to do?

During Bath Time

◆

Let's Ponder

How did the dinosaurs clean themselves?

How did the idea of a rubber ducky in the bath first begin?

How would a queen's bathtub look? Why?

How do astronauts flying in space clean themselves?

Why do people usually bathe their dogs, but not their cats?

How would you get your dog to stay still during his bath?

How would you make sure soap did not get in your child's eyes during bath time?

Let's Compare

How are a bathtub and a swimming pool alike? How are they different?

How are shampoo and soap alike? How are they different?

How are a bar of soap and a cube of ice alike? How are they different?

Let's Decide

Who should decide when it is time to take a bath? Why?

Are baths better to take in the morning or at night? Why?

Which do you prefer — a shower or a bath? Why?

Which body part gets dirtier faster than any other part? Why?

Do kids like to be dirty? Why or why not?

Do gorillas like to take baths? Why or why not?

Will the way bathtubs look and work ever change? Why or why not?

Let's Imagine

Something other than water is coming out of your bathtub faucet. What is coming out and why?

You are the parent and your child never wants to take a bath. How could you make bath time more fun?

You have invented a way to get clean without using any soap or water. How does your invention work?

Approaching Bedtime

◆

Let's Ponder

Why do so many kids enjoy hearing a bedtime story?

Where would be a very strange place to sleep?

What is a good activity to do before going to bed? Why?

Why do some people have trouble falling asleep?

Why do people often have trouble remembering their dreams?

Why do some people need less sleep than others?

Why do many kids resist going to bed?

Let's Compare

How are blankets and sheets alike? How are they different?

How are your parents' bed and your bed alike? How are they different?

How are your daydreams and your dreams while you sleep alike? How are they different?

Let's Decide

Is it good to have a bedtime? Why or why not?

Who should decide when it is time to go to bed? Why?

Do dogs dream? Why or why not?

What was your favorite dream ever about? Why was it your favorite?

What was your worst nightmare about? Why was it so frightening to you?

Do adult dogs have a bedtime for their puppies? Why or why not?

Did cave people have a bedtime for their children? Why or why not?

Let's Imagine

You have invented a dream machine. What does it look like? How does it work?

You have invented a snore-stopper gadget. What does it look like? How does it work?

You have just awakened after sleeping for one hundred years. What has changed while you were asleep?

Away from Home

◆

Riding in the Car

◆

Let's Ponder

Why won't some people wear their seat belts even
though they have been proven to save lives?

Why would school buses be allowed to operate without seat belts?

What might be dangerous about a child yelling in the
car?

What other types of transportation do people use
besides cars?

What could you do to make the time of a long car
ride seem faster?

How would your life be different if there suddenly
were no cars?

What would the inside of a president's car look like?

Let's Compare

How are riding a bike and driving a car alike? How
are they different?

How are windshield wipers and a broom alike? How
are they different?

How are the car seat and a living room couch alike?
How are they different?

Let's Decide

Would you like to have a TV in your car? Why or
why not?

What is your favorite kind of car? Why?

Where is your favorite place to sit in the car? Why?

Do you like convertibles? Why or why not?

Will roads still look the same when you are a grand-parent? Why or why not?

What age do you think is a good age to learn to drive? Why?

Should pets wear seat belts when they ride in a car? Why or why not?

Let's Imagine

A new law has been passed allowing pigs to drive. What does a pig car look like?

The horn on your new car doesn't beep or honk. What does it do instead?

You are riding in the car of the richest person in the world. How does it look on the inside and outside?

Arriving at Grandma's and Grandpa's

◆

Let's Ponder

What do grandparents like best about being grand-parents?

What do grandparents wish for their grandchildren?

What might make a grandparent sad? Why?

What might frustrate a grandparent? Why?

What might frighten a grandparent? Why?

What makes your grandmother special?

What makes your grandfather special?

Let's Compare

How are your grandparents and your parents alike? How are they different?

How are your house and your grandparents' house alike? How are they different?

How are your grandfather's clothes and your father's clothes alike? How are they different?

Let's Decide

Should your grandparents have to follow your parents' rules? Why or why not?

What do grandparents like the most when their grandchildren come and visit?

Should grandparents live with their grandchildren? Why or why not?

What makes a good grandparent? Why?

Which of your books would have been your grandmother's favorite when she was your age? Why?

Which of your books would have been your grandfather's favorite when he was your age? Why?

Do grandparents prefer the world today or how it was when they were young? Why?

Let's Imagine

Your grandchildren are coming to visit. What will you do with them?

Instead of a milk shake, your grandfather drank the new grandpa shake. What happened after he drank it?

Your grandmother just won first prize in the Boogie Woogie Grandma Dance Contest. Show me the dance she did.

Playing at the Beach

◆

Let's Ponder

How do you think the idea of surfing first came about?

What would be very strange to see at the beach?

Where else can you find sand besides at the beach?

Why are oceans salty, but rivers not salty?

What could you add to a sand castle that would make it extra special?

Why do seagulls like to fly over the ocean and sand?

Why might someone not like the beach?

Let's Compare

How are waves and the wind alike? How are they different?

How are lifeguards and firefighters alike? How are they different?

How are a lake and an ocean alike? How are they different?

Let's Decide

Do you like to go to the beach? Why or why not?

Should dogs be allowed on the beach? Why or why not?

What would you pack for a picnic lunch on the beach?

Is beach sand the same as desert sand? Why or why not?

Do babies like the beach? Why or why not?

What would be ridiculous to wear to the beach?

Do fish like people swimming in the ocean? Why or why not?

Let's Imagine

Something very strange occurred when you put on your new suntan lotion. What happened?

You found a sunken treasure chest that had been buried on the ocean floor. What was inside when you opened it up?

A mermaid has just popped out of the sea to ask you a question. What does she want to know?

Enjoying the Park

◆

Let's Ponder

Where else besides parks are drinking fountains found?

If a slide could talk, what would it say?

If the swings could talk, what would they say?

Why do you think people call it a park?

What else could you call a park?

How will parks look one hundred years from now?

Why do most kids enjoy the park?

Let's Compare

How are a park and a backyard alike? How are they different?

How are a slide and a ramp alike? How are they different?

How are monkey bars and crib bars alike? How are
they different?

Let's Decide

What is your favorite thing to do at the park?

Which park equipment is the most difficult for adults
to play on? Why?

On which park equipment do most accidents occur?
Why?

Do monkeys really know how to cross the monkey
bars? Why or why not?

What makes a park pretty?

What is the best park you have ever played at? Why?

Who is responsible for keeping a park clean?

Let's Imagine

You have landed on the planet Figloggy. What do the
parks look like? What kind of equipment do they
have?

Your city has built a park for adults only. What does
it look like? What kind of equipment does it have?

Your city has built a park especially for dogs. What
does it look like? What kind of equipment does it
have?

Strolling Through the Zoo

◆

Let's Ponder

What else besides animals can be seen at the zoo?

Why do most kids like the zoo?

Why might someone think zoos are cruel to animals?

Why might someone think zoos are not cruel to animals?

Why do just giraffes have such long necks?

How did the idea for zoos first begin?

Why are so many people terrified of snakes?

Let's Compare

How are gorillas and humans alike? How are they different?

How are an elephant's nose and a garden hose alike? How are they different?

How are an animal trainer and a ballet teacher alike? How are they different?

Let's Decide

Could lions survive in the jungle after living in a zoo? Why or why not?

Would animals choose to live in a zoo or jungle? Why?

Would animals enjoy strolling through a human zoo? Why or why not?

What is your favorite zoo animal? Why?

Which zoo animal probably eats the most food?

Would you like to be a zookeeper? Why or why not?

Would you like to be an animal trainer? Why or why not?

Let's Imagine

One of your favorite zoo animals is having a conversation with you. Which animal is it? What are you talking about?

All the rattlesnake cages are open and empty! As the zookeeper, what are you going to do to warn people without causing everyone to scream and panic?

The gorillas are demanding to eat something other than bananas. What do they want and why?

Smiling at the Circus

◆

Let's Ponder

What would a lion tamer need to know in order to train lions?

How do you think lion tamers make sure they are safe while working with lions?

Why might someone not enjoy watching animals perform tricks?

What might be difficult about being a clown?

What did the first clown look like and do?

How would you describe the circus to someone who is blind?

How might circuses be different one hundred years from now?

Let's Compare

How are a trapeze and a swing at the park alike? How are they different?

How are the circus and the zoo alike? How are they different?

How are the ringmaster and the general of an army alike? How are they different?

Let's Decide

Do animals like to perform tricks? Why or why not?

Are lions afraid to jump through hoops on fire? Why or why not?

Would you like to swing from a trapeze? Why or why not?

Would you like to walk on the high rope? Why or why not?

Would you like to be a clown? Why or why not?

Which circus animal is the smartest? Why?

What is your favorite part of the circus?

Let's Imagine

You have taught an elephant a trick that no other elephant has ever done. What is the trick?

Amazingly, the lions have taught their trainer to do a trick. What did they teach him?

The clowns are making everyone cry instead of laugh. What is going on?

Browsing at the Library

◆

Let's Ponder

How might an adult's life be different if he or she could not read?

Why don't some kids like to read?

How would you get a child interested in reading?

What else besides videos and tapes will be available at libraries in the future?

What else could a library be called?

What would a librarian need to know in order to do her job?

How can books help people?

Let's Compare

How are a book and a magazine alike? How are they different?

How are reading a book and singing a song alike? How are they different?

How are a book cover and clothing alike? How are they different?

Let's Decide

Would a dog want to read a book about humans? Why or why not?

What is your favorite book? Why?

Do you prefer books with lots of pictures? Why or why not?

Would you want someone to write a book about you? Why or why not?

If you could pick one story character to come alive and spend the day with you, who would it be? Why?

How many books a week do you think kids should read or hear?

Is it really important to be quiet at the library? Why or why not?

Let's Imagine

You are a famous author. What is the name of your book? What is it about?

Only one book is left in the world. What happened to
all the other books?

A spaceship is parked in front of the library. What is
going on?

Going to the Toy Store

♦

Let's Ponder

What would a person need to know to make toys?

Why do a lot of kids like to play with model cars?

Why might some kids not like to share their toys?

How would you teach your child about sharing his or
her toys with other children?

Why might some parents think it is wrong for children to play with toy weapons?

Why might some parents think it is fine for children
to play with toy weapons?

Let's Compare

How are a dollhouse and your home alike? How are
they different?

How are roller skates and a skateboard alike? How
are they different?

How are a Frisbee and a dinner plate alike? How are
they different?

Let's Decide

What toy would children all over the world like to
play with? Why?

What is your favorite toy? Why?

Which of your toys would an adult like to play with? Why?

If you could pick one of your toys to come alive, what would you pick? Why?

Do television commercials influence kids to buy toys? Why or why not?

Do kids who own only a few toys have a better imagination? Why or why not?

If you could buy five things in a toy store, what would you choose?

Let's Imagine

You have invented a very popular toy for adults. What does it look like? How do adults play with it?

The children on the planet Sneezewhallo play with a very strange kind of toy. What does it look like? How do they play with it?

You have discovered the very first toy that ever appeared on this planet. What does it look like? How did kids play with it?

Shopping at the Supermarket

◆

Let's Ponder

What would cave dwellers think about our huge supermarkets?

What could a supermarket have to entertain kids as they wait in long checkout lines?

What kinds of things should not be allowed in a supermarket? Why?

What else besides food can be found in a supermarket?

What would a supermarket checker have to know in order to do his or her job?

What goes on late at night in a supermarket after it has closed?

What would be the most difficult thing about owning a supermarket? Why?

Let's Compare

How are grocery carts and wagons alike? How are they different?

How are shopping for food and shopping for clothes alike? How are they different?

How are grocery sacks and pillowcases alike? How are they different?

Let's Decide

Do you like to go grocery shopping? Why or why not?

Who should do the grocery shopping? Why?

Which food item is bought the most often? Why?

Which food item is bought the least often? Why?

What is the most expensive item at the supermarket?

Which is your favorite aisle in the supermarket? Why?

Would you like to own a supermarket? Why or why not?

Let's Imagine

While you are grocery shopping, the food in your basket begins to talk to you. What is it saying? What do you answer?

On Third Street, there is a grocery store for cats only. What is inside the store? What do the shopping carts look like?

One hundred years from now, supermarkets have an aisle called Space Food. What does space food look like? How does it taste?

Waiting at the Doctor's

♦

Let's Ponder

Why would a person want to become a doctor?

What would a person have to study to become a doctor?

What would a person have to study to become a nurse?

How did doctors and nurses come to wear white?

What might make a doctor nervous? Why?

Why are some people frightened by the sight of blood?

Why do doctors charge so much money?

Let's Compare

How are a doctor and a mother alike? How are they different?

How are a doctor and a car mechanic alike? How are they different?

How is getting a shot and being pricked by a rose thorn alike? How are they different?

Let's Decide

Do you prefer a male or female doctor? Why?

Would you like to be a doctor? Why or why not?

Would you like to be a nurse? Why or why not?

What is the most difficult thing a doctor does? Why?

Should doctors help people even if they don't have any money to pay for the visit? Why or why not?

Could a deaf person be a doctor? Why or why not?

Do doctors take care of themselves or do they go to another doctor when they become ill? Why?

Let's Imagine

One hundred years from now people will take their temperature in a very different way. What will they use? How will it show a person's temperature?

Your child is very nervous about seeing the doctor. How will you help him or her relax?

You are asked to design the waiting room of a doctor's office. What will it look like?

Visiting the Dentist

◆

Let's Ponder

How would you make brushing teeth fun for children?

What else besides toothbrushes have bristles?

What are some things that could hurt a tooth?

What would a dentist need to know in order to do his or her job?

How would your life be different if you had no teeth?

Why do you think only humans — and not other animals — brush their teeth?

How do you think the idea of toothpaste first began?

Let's Compare

How are losing a tooth and losing a friend alike? How are they different?

How are a cavity and a paper cut alike? How are they different?

How are a dentist and a hairdresser alike? How are they different?

Let's Decide

Would you like to be a dentist? Why or why not?

Could a deaf person be a dentist? Why or why not?

What does a dentist enjoy most about his or her job?

What does a dentist enjoy least about his or her job?

Who dislikes going to the dentist the most — adults or kids? Why?

Do people from all over the world care for their teeth in the same way? Why or why not?

Do you believe in the tooth fairy? Why or why not?

Let's Imagine

You are known as the fun dentist. What do you do that makes kids want to visit you?

You have created a toothbrush for sharks. What does it look like? How do the sharks use it?

You are the dentist and a little girl bites you every time you put your hand in her mouth. What are you going to do?

Sitting at the Airport

◆

Let's Ponder

What would you put in airport terminals to make the waiting go faster?

What would a pilot have to learn in order to fly a plane?

Why do you think people didn't invent airplanes until just about a hundred years ago?

What would the birds say to the planes passing by if they could talk?

What other things besides planes fly in the sky?

What would the inside of a president's plane look like?

What animals might be frightened by flying in a plane? Why?

Let's Compare

How are a plane and a bird alike? How are they different?

How are a pilot and a bus driver alike? How are they different?

How are a flight attendant and a waitress alike? How are they different?

Let's Decide

Would you like to be a flight attendant? Why or why not?

Would you like to be an airline pilot? Why or why not?

If you could pick anywhere in the world, where would you want to fly? Why?

Do you prefer to travel by plane or train? Why?

Why are airplane tickets so expensive?

Will people still be traveling in airplanes one hundred years from now? Why or why not?

Should a pilot be able to fly again if he or she has crashed another plane? Why or why not?

Let's Imagine

You just opened your suitcase and your clothes are all gone! What's packed in place of your clothes?

Your plane has just made an emergency landing on a small island in the middle of nowhere. What does the island look like? Who lives there?

You are the boss of an airline for pets. What do your pet planes look like? What do you do to make sure the animals are comfortable throughout each flight?

Camping Outdoors

♦

Let's Ponder

Why might someone want to go camping?

Why might someone not want to go camping?

What do you think forest animals think of campers? Why?

Why do you think some campers litter?

How would you convince someone to protect a forest?

How would you show a deer that there is no reason to be afraid of you?

What kinds of food are not wise to bring camping? Why?

Let's Compare

How are a sleeping bag and a bed alike? How are they different?

How are a tent and a house alike? How are they different?

How are a hiking trail and a highway road alike? How are they different?

Let's Decide

Should big camping vehicles be allowed in campgrounds? Why or why not?

Should televisions be allowed in campgrounds? Why or why not?

What is the most important thing to bring camping? Why?

Do you like to go hiking? Why or why not?

Which forest animal would you like to see while camping? Why?

Which forest animal would you prefer not to see while camping? Why?

Would you rather sleep in a bed or a sleeping bag? Why?

Let's Imagine

You have invented a new tent that has something no other tent has. What is so special about your tent?

You open your tent door and see a big bear eating all your food! What are you going to do?

A forest animal has decided to become your pet. Which animal is it? What did you do to make it want to stay with you?

On Special Occasions

◆

The First Day of School

◆

Let's Ponder

Why do some kids get nervous on their first day of school?

What would you say to your child to help him or her not be so nervous?

What else besides lunch boxes and paper sacks could be used to carry a lunch?

What would be embarrassing to wear to school? Why?

Why do some kids love to go to school?

Why do some kids hate to go to school?

How would you change school so that more kids would like it?

Let's Compare

How are teachers and parents alike? How are they different?

How are teachers and baby-sitters alike? How are they different?

How are a school backpack and a purse alike? How are they different?

Let's Decide

Do teachers get nervous on the first day of school? Why or why not?

Do parents get nervous on their children's first day of school? Why or why not?

What would be the best lunch to have on the first day of school? Why?

Would you rather walk or take a school bus? Why?

Do you prefer a male or female teacher? Why?

Do you prefer a young or old teacher? Why?

Do teachers have favorite students? Why or why not?

Let's Imagine

You are the teacher and all of the students are out of their seats and running around. What will you do?

You walk into your classroom and discover that the students are not humans. Who (or what) is sitting at the desks?

You are in charge of what the students in your class will learn this year. What will you teach them?

The First Snowy Day

◆

Let's Ponder

How would you describe snow to someone who has never seen or felt it?

How would winter be different if snow were black instead of white?

What else besides snowmen can be built out of snow?

How would you make a snow<u>lady</u> out of snow?

What are some things that are not fun to do in the snow?

What animals would enjoy the snow? Why?

What animals would not enjoy the snow? Why?

Let's Compare

How are a scarecrow and a snowman alike? How are they different?

How are snow and rain alike? How are they different?

How are playing with sand and playing with snow alike? How are they different?

Let's Decide

What is your favorite thing to do in the snow?

Would you rather be inside or outside when it is snowing? Why?

Who likes the snow the most — adults or kids? Why?

What is a good snack after playing in the snow on a cold winter day?

Would you like to live in a place where it never snows? Why or why not?

Would you like to live in a place where it snows all year long? Why or why not?

Do you think it snows on planets in other galaxies? Why or why not?

Let's Imagine

Last night a magical snow fell. What happened when it touched the ground?

You have invented a snowbike. What does it look like? How can a child ride it in the snow?

The snow falling from the sky is sticking to you

like glue! What is going on? What are you going
to do?

The First Day of Spring

◆

Let's Ponder

What could be used to make a strange tail for a kite?

How do you think the idea for the first kite came
about?

Why do kids think it's fun to splash in puddles?

What cartoon characters would enjoy springtime?
Why?

What kinds of things would you like to plant in the
spring?

Why do you think this season is called "spring"?

What other names could be given to this time of year?

Let's Compare

How are spring and summer alike? How are they different?

How are a butterfly and a bird alike? How are they
different?

How are the petals of a flower and the leaves of a tree
alike? How are they different?

Let's Decide

What is your favorite flower? Why?

Should people be allowed to catch butterflies? Why or
why not?

Do you like flying a kite? Why or why not?

What do adults like most about spring? Why?

What do kids like most about spring? Why?

Do you like rainy days? Why or why not?

Should kids be allowed to play in the rain? Why or why not?

Let's Imagine

You have just seen a new butterfly that no one else has ever seen. What does it look like?

On a weird spring day, something other than raindrops is falling from the clouds. What is coming out of the clouds? What is going on?

You have been asked to plant a garden for the three little pigs. What will you plant?

A Birthday

◆

Let's Ponder

Why won't some adults tell their age on their birthday?

How would you celebrate your birthday if you had no money?

How could you wrap a birthday present if there were no wrapping paper or bags left in the world?

How does Mary Poppins celebrate her birthday?

What kind of presents does Minnie Mouse receive on her birthday?

What would be some strange gifts to give a mother on her birthday?

What might make a child sad on his or her birthday?

Let's Compare

How are wrapping paper and newspaper alike? How are they different?

How are frosting and shaving cream alike? How are they different?

How are inflated and deflated balloons alike? How are they different?

Let's Decide

Do you like getting dressed up for birthday parties? Why or why not?

Is celebrating a birthday important to adults? Why or why not?

What has been your favorite birthday? Why?

Which do you prefer to receive on your birthday — toys, money, or clothes? Why?

What did Bugs Bunny wish for when he blew out his birthday candles?

What was the best birthday gift you ever received? Why?

What was the worst birthday gift you ever received? Why?

Let's Imagine

You are in charge of planning a birthday party for your pet dog. What will the guests do? What will you serve to eat?

You are in charge of planning a birthday party for yourself. What will the guests do? What will you serve to eat?

You made the cake for the queen's birthday. What does it look like?

Halloween

◆

Let's Ponder

What else besides candy can people give out on Halloween?

What would you teach your children to make sure that they were safe on Halloween?

What would you use to make a costume if you had no money?

How do you think a jack-o'-lantern first got its name?

What else can be carved besides pumpkins?

Why might some people think bats are scary?

Why do some kids like to scare others?

Let's Compare

How are a witch and a vampire alike? How are they different?

How are a witch's hat and a visor alike? How are they different?

How are trick-or-treaters and actors in a play alike? How are they different?

Let's Decide

What is the scariest costume you have ever seen?

What kind of costume would you never want to wear? Why?

Do you believe that some houses are haunted? Why or why not?

Which do you enjoy more—Halloween or the Fourth of July? Why?

Would adults like to dress up and go trick-or-treating? Why or why not?

What would your father choose for a costume? Why?

What would your mother choose for a costume? Why?

Let's Imagine

You are a famous reporter assigned to ask a vampire four questions. What are they?

You wake up and see a ghost on the end of your bed. Why is it there?

On Halloween morning you discover that you are walking around in your skeleton! What is going on? What are your going to do?

Thanksgiving Day

◆

Let's Ponder

Why aren't some people thankful for what they have?

How do you show others when you are thankful for something they have done?

What could Native Americans at the first Thanksgiving teach people today?

What else has the same texture as pumpkin pie?

What kind of food would be very unusual to serve on Thanksgiving?

Why might someone think having a large Thanksgiving feast is wrong?

Why might someone think having a large Thanksgiving feast is important?

Let's Compare

How are cranberries and cherries alike? How are they different?

How are the stuffing in a pillow and the stuffing in a turkey alike? How are they different?

How are the crust of a pie and the crust of the earth alike? How are they different?

Let's Decide

What is your favorite Thanksgiving food?

Do all countries have a day for giving thanks? Why or why not?

Would you have liked to be a Pilgrim at the first Thanksgiving? Why or why not?

Would you like to wear clothing like the Pilgrims? Why or why not?

What are your parents most thankful for?

What are you most thankful for?

What is Miss Piggy most thankful for?

Let's Imagine

The talking turkeys on Mr. Strange-o's turkey farm are trying to convince Mr. Strange-o not to cook them for Thanksgiving. What are they saying? What will Mr. Strange-o answer?

This Thanksgiving the turkey is stuffed with something very strange! What is it stuffed with? How did it get inside the turkey?

It is the first Thanksgiving and you have been asked to say grace. What will you say?

Valentine's Day

◆

Let's Ponder

Why is the heart used as the symbol to show love?

What would be a very unusual valentine? Why?

What can people do to show others that they care about them?

Why do some kids like to tease others about their girlfriends and boyfriends?

What other things sound like a kiss?

How do you think giving candy on Valentine's Day first began?

What do very rich people give their sweethearts on Valentine's Day?

Let's Compare

How are a birthday card and a valentine card alike? How are they different?

How are a kiss and a handshake alike? How are they different?

How are Valentine's Day and a wedding anniversary alike? How are they different?

Let's Decide

Which famous person would you like to receive a valentine from? Why?

Which do you think are better — homemade or store-bought valentines? Why?

Should kids give valentines to all or just some of the kids in their class? Why?

Should people give valentines to their pets?

Is it better to show or to tell people that you love them? Why?

Is Valentine's Day an important holiday? Why or why not?

What would you like to receive on Valentine's Day?

Let's Imagine

You received the funniest valentine. What does it look like?

You received the ugliest valentine. What does it look like?

You received the prettiest valentine. What does it look like?

The Fourth of July

♦

Let's Ponder

Why do you think Betsy Ross chose red and white stripes to sew on the American flag?

What would the American flag look like if you had been chosen to sew it?

What things sound louder than fireworks?

Why are some dogs frightened by fireworks while other dogs are not?

Why are some people willing to risk their lives in order to have freedom?

Why do many different celebrations display fireworks?

What are you free to do that children in other countries are not?

Let's Compare

How are fireworks and rockets alike? How are they different?

How are the birthday of a country and the birthday of a person alike? How are they different?

How are parades and fashion shows alike? How are they different?

Let's Decide

Is it important to celebrate the birth of a country? Why or why not?

Do countries all over the world celebrate the birth of their nation? Why or why not?

Should one country rule over another? Why or why not?

Would you be willing to fight for your country's freedom if it were ruled by another? Why or why not?

What would you want to wear and do if you could be in a Fourth of July parade?

Who should be allowed to set off fireworks? Why?

What would you choose to eat at a Fourth of July picnic?

Let's Imagine

The American flag has just spoken to you. What did it say? Why did it choose to talk to you and no one else?

This strange Fourth of July the sky is filled with something other than fireworks. What is in the sky? How are the people reacting?

The Fourth of July has been changed to the Fourth of December. What changes might occur now that this holiday is in the middle of winter?

Formula II:

Creating Your Own Thinking Questions

By simply following the same formula used in Part II, you can create your own thought-provoking questions. These open-ended questions are divided into four categories. Children are asked to:

Ponder Ask questions that prompt children to wonder about the origin of events, inventions, and words; how specific objects and customs may change in the future; why events and objects may appear differently to other people; and how things might appear or work differently after certain changes.

Example: How did socks get their name?

Compare Ask questions that prompt a comparison between two different objects or actions.

Example: How is getting dressed like wrapping a gift?

Decide Ask questions that require a decision about something, and then challenge children to support their answer with reasons.

Example: Could a plant be a friend? Why or why not?

Imagine Describe a new and different situation, and then ask children questions that challenge them to elaborate on what you have presented.

Example: You have invented a way to get clean without using any soap or water. How does your invention work?

These four categories can be easily remembered by referring to the acronym PCDI (Ponder, Compare, Decide, Imagine).

Practice

The following exercises will help you become more familiar with Formula II. Although the words in the blank spaces of the exercises will change, these basic questions can be asked over and over again.

Have fun as you try the exercises. And remember — there are no wrong answers!

Exercise I:

Comparing Questions

These kinds of questions (e.g., How are dogs like cats? How are hands and feet different?) can be asked throughout the day. To create such questions, look for similarities and differences in your child's surroundings. Write these ideas and more in the blanks below.

Example: How are <u>bicyles</u> like <u>cars</u>?

How are _____like

_____?

How are _____and

_____different?

Exercise II:

Deciding Questions

These kinds of questions (e.g., What is your favorite toy? What is the best way to build a sand castle? Is it really important to take a bath every day?) can prompt children to reflect upon their surroundings and activities. To create such questions, think of things that your child is likely to have an opinion about. Write these ideas and more in the blanks below.

Example: What is the best <u>movie</u> you ever <u>saw?</u> Why?

What is your favorite _____? Why?

Do you like _____? Why or why not? _____

What is the best you ever _____? Why?

Who should be responsible for _____?
   Why?

Would you like to be a _____?
   Why or why not?

Is it really important to _____?
   Why or why not?

Could a deaf person _____?
   Why or why not?

Do you prefer _____
   or _____?
   Why?

Exercise III:

Imagining Questions

These kinds of questions (e.g., You have created a new toy. What does it look like? How does it work? You are the parent. How will you get your children to quit fighting? You have just seen a kind of bird that no one else has seen. What does it look like? Why hasn't anyone ever seen it before?) can stimulate your child's imagination throughout the day. To create such questions, just think of events, people, animals, and objects in your child's life. Write these ideas and more in the blanks below.

Example: You own a very strange dog. What happens every time it barks?

You have created a new _____. What does it look like? How does it work?

On the planet Weirdleeda, they do not use _____ _____for _____. _____ What do they use instead?

You tried to _____, but everything went wrong. What happened?

You are the parent. How will you get your children to _____?

You have just seen a _____ that no one else has seen. What does it look like?

You own a very strange _____. What happens when it _____?

Exercise IV:

Pondering Questions

These kinds of questions (e.g., What else could bananas be called? Why? What will refrigerators look like one hundred years from now? How would a queen's bathtub look?) can prompt your child to think of ordinary objects and events in a new and different way. To create such questions, think of things your child plays with, enjoys, and is interested in. Write these ideas and more in the blanks below.

Example: How would you describe a rainbow to someone who is blind?

What else could _____

    be called? Why?

How would _____

    be different if _____?

How do you think _____

    began?

How would a queen's _____

    look? Why?

What would be very strange to _____?

    Why?

How would your life be different if there were no _____?

What will _____

    look like one hundred years from now?

How would you describe _____

    to someone who is blind?

Index

◆